THE GOSPEL OF MARK: LIVE

Richard Ramsey, PhD

The author's own translation appears in italic type.

Edited by Rena Bell Yeager, Pixley Knob Press
Cover design by Kendall Unrau

Print ISBN - 979-8-9950028-0-2
Ebook ISBN - 979-8-9950028-1-9

To Mom and Dad, who live the gospel.

CONTENTS

INTRODUCTION

Mark is the master storyteller. The pace is extraordinary. Jesus is constantly on the move. Mark is a ninety minute narrative that was likely conveyed orally before it was written. Jesus is always teaching in Mark, yet rather than sermons, Mark reveals Jesus by way of miracles, controversies, and personal encounters. Thus, it is half the length of the other gospels but has the most miracles. Mark highlights the emotional side of Jesus leading a passionate ministry. The reader is confronted with the visceral depth of Jesus' convictions. Jesus displays severe anger, shock, and dread as He relentlessly pursues His Father's calling in an evil world.

Upon first encounter, Mark may appear to be an assortment of random episodes in the life of Jesus. Yet, Mark is deeply structured and intentionally theological. This book contains my rudimentary translation of the entire gospel. My translation is more literal, particularly the verb tenses. Mark, originally written in Greek, made frequent use of the historical present tense. Rather than saying (as most translations do) in Mark 9:2 "Jesus took Peter, James, and John and brought them up the mountain." The text literally reads, "Jesus takes along Peter, James, and John and brings them up the mountain." This storytelling technique is to give the reader/hearer a sense of being a co-witness to the story, to visualize the action. While it doesn't make for the most proper literature, it vividly animates the story.

While the storytelling technique is engaging, it serves a more eternal purpose. The gospel is not simply a history or biography of Jesus. It is a proclamation to hear and accept the truth of Jesus as God's anointed one to bring people to the Father by faith and become a disciple in Christ's kingdom. The gospel lays claims on all those who hear or read it. The first words of Jesus are, "The time has come, the kingdom of God has drawn near, repent and believe the good news." Thus, the responsibility of knowing the truth puts everyone in God's plan. One may be a follower who may struggle and fail, but perseveres and bears fruit. One may be prideful, concerned mainly with power, money, and distractions. The gospel gives continual warnings and examples of both the disciple and the one who, for whatever reason, refuses to follow.

The translation is divided up into sections in italicized font, followed by as brief an explanation as possible. The brevity allows the reader to continue reading Mark as a whole, to understand the core message, consider the claims, see yourself in the story, and see how the message of the gospel progresses and builds with each section. A very oversimplified outline is that Jesus starts by establishing His identity, then defines faith according to His kingdom, then defines discipleship, and finally what serving and suffering may be called for in discipleship. These four major movements, in that order each cover roughly a fourth of the gospel.

There are many great books written on the gospel of Mark. The three below are excellent and extensive, each being several hundred pages worth reading for further study.

Edwards, James. The Gospel According to Mark. Eerdmans, 2001.

Garland, David. Mark. Zondervan Academic,1996.

Stein, Robert. Mark. Baker 2008.

However, this much shorter and less technical book hopes to take you through the gospel in one sitting if you desire. To see the entire landscape of the life and calling of Jesus in a few hours. However, regardless of your reading pace, is the faithfulness to His calling to "believe the good news."

Finally, who was Mark? Mark traveled with Paul and Barnabus on Paul's first missionary journey. He did not complete the journey and later Paul and Barnabus split over whether or not to take Mark on the next journey. Barnabus took Mark and Paul then chose Silas (Acts 15). Yet in what is believed to be Paul's last chapter of his last letter, he asks Timothy to bring Mark with him when he comes for he was helpful in ministry (2 Timothy 4:11). Mark was also Peter's companion throughout Peter's ministry. It is believed that most material from Mark originated with Peter. There are various ancient traditions concerning the rest of Mark's life and ministry. This gospel is what we have for certain, for us to encounter the Son of God.

CHAPTER ONE

The beginning of the gospel of Jesus Christ, the Son of God, As it was written in the prophets, "See, I will send my messenger ahead of you to prepare your way. The voice crying in the desert, make his paths straight." John the Baptist came baptizing and preaching in the desert, a baptism of repentance for the forgiveness of sins.

The whole region of Judea and Jerusalem went out to him confessing their sins, and he baptized them in the Jordan river. John wore camel's hair with a leather belt around his waist, and ate locusts and wild honey. He was preaching, "One greater than me is coming, I'm unfit to stoop down and untie his sandals. I baptized you with water, he will baptize you with the Holy Spirit!" 1-8

No stable or wise men. The first line ... "Jesus is the Christ," or "messiah" in Hebrew. He is the anointed long awaited savior the Old Testament promised. More than that, He is the Son of God. We know his identity from the beginning and He will prove it with his life. John the Baptist is given a quick intro, his clothing identifies him as the "Elijah who was to come" (Malachi 4:5-6) before the messiah. His diet tells us he is a desert prophet. His main message is not about himself, keeping the traditions of the past, or even a new teaching, but to be on the lookout for the messiah. He would lead a great revival of repentance. Even so, the people would not be prepared for this messiah.

> *And then in those days, Jesus came from Nazareth in Galilee and was baptized in the Jordan by John. Immediately going up out of the water, he saw the heavens tearing open and the Spirit descending like a dove upon him. A voice came from heaven, "You are my Son, I love, in you I am well pleased." And immediately, the Spirit drove him into the desert for forty days, being tempted by Satan, he was with the wild animals and angels ministered to him.*
>
> *Then later, when John was imprisoned, Jesus came into Galilee proclaiming the gospel of God, "The time has come, the kingdom of God has drawn near, repent and believe the good news." 9-15*

In rapid fire Jesus is baptized, tempted, and starts preaching. In the Baptism we see a rare glimpse of the Trinity. While John had baptized the masses for repentance, this baptism was to affirm Jesus as the Christ. Rather than a parade or coronation, he goes straight to fasting in the desert with Satan, He overcomes the temptation and is prepared for ministry. He returns to preach the basic prophetic message John started. The time for the kingdom to break forth has come – repent and believe. He will spend the rest of the gospel expanding on exactly what repentance and faith require.

> *And passing by the Sea of Galilee, He saw Simon and his brother Andrew casting a net into the sea; they were fishermen. He said to them, "Come follow me and I will make you fishers of men." Immediately they left their nets and followed him.*
>
> *Going a little further he saw James the son of Zebedee and his brother John mending their nets. Immediately he called them and they left their father in the boat with the hired men and went with Him. 16-20*

Jesus has begun His Message, "Repent and Believe, the Kingdom is here." Yet focus quickly goes to gathering disciples. These first four were devout Jewish fishermen. Jesus did not need "help" so much as he was to start a disciple making movement among people. He would make disciples who would make disciples. Not the typical recruiting pool to start a movement.

But Jesus knew exactly who he was calling, these men would be able to reach real people with the message of Jesus in a way the elites or powerful would not attempt. The fact they left the family business demonstrates their readiness to follow. They will fail many times in understanding and practicing their faith, yet will ultimately persevere. All followers will have this struggle.

> *They went into Capernaum and immediately on the Sabbath entered the synagogue. Jesus was teaching and they were astonished as his teaching was with authority, not like the scribes.*
>
> *Immediately there was in the synagogue a man with*

> *an evil spirit who cried out, "What business do we have, Jesus of Nazareth? Did you come to destroy us? I know you are the Holy one of God." Jesus rebuked him saying, "Be Silent and come out of him!" The spirit convulsed him, and crying loudly came out of him.*
>
> *All were astonished and asked themselves, "What is this new teaching? He commands evil spirits with authority and they obey him. Immediately the news about Him spread everywhere in the region of Galilee. 21-28*

The Synagogue is the all-purpose meeting place for Jewish life every Sabbath. Here we see Jesus teaching. Rather than a transcript of his sermon, we have the interruption. How many weeks had this demon possessed man likely been in the synagogue, unthreatened by the teachings of the Jewish leaders. But with Jesus, the demon breaks into an uncontrollable fit. The first phrase is a figure of speech literally, "what to us and to you"? It is a forceful protest of being in proximity of one another.

The demon then asks if it will be destroyed. Jesus just having defeated Satan at the temptation surely has a reputation among the demons and they are in fear. The demon concludes its speech by giving Jesus his rightful identity, "The Holy One of God."

In response, Jesus refuses conversation, and is only concerned with freeing the man from its torment. This is the authority accompanying his teaching that awes the congregation, and the awe quickly spreads. In one short encounter, Mark reveals Jesus has supernatural power over evil.

Immediately upon leaving the Synagogue, He went to Simon and Andrew's house with James and John. Simon's mother-in-law lay sick with a fever. Immediately they told Jesus about it and He went to her, taking her hand to help her up. The fever left her and she began to serve them.

That night they brought all the sick and demon possessed, the whole town at the door. He healed various diseases and drove out many demons, but He would not let the demons speak since they knew He was the Christ. 29-34

Peter's home will become a homebase for Jesus during His ministry. His mother-in-law, possibly the matriarch, is sick. Of all the times to be sick in bed when you literally have Jesus coming for dinner? This healing is not as "exciting" as the exorcism, yet what is highlighted is not simply Jesus' compassion, but her response. When Jesus heals the response is to serve. She has the honor of demonstrating this discipleship pattern.

We then see the crowd gathering for healing and exorcism; how fast the news has spread. Jesus puts on a spiritual clinic of healing and freeing from demons. He does not let demons speak. Often referred to as the "Markan secret," Jesus will control how He is revealed and who his messengers will be. The demons do not make the cut.

Rising early, well before sunrise, He went out to a private place and was praying. Simon and those with Him searched for Him and having found Him said, "Everyone is looking for You"! He replied, "Come, let's go somewhere else. To the neighboring towns so I can preach, that is why I have come."

And He went preaching and casting out demons throughout the synagogues of Galilee. A leper comes to Him begging and kneeling down saying, "If You are willing, You are able to cleanse me." Moved with compassion, He touched him and said, I am willing, be clean."

Immediately the leprosy was healed and he was clean. He sternly warned him saying "Say nothing about this, but go show yourself to the priest and offer the sacrifice Moses commanded for your cleansing for a testimony to them." Yet he was going out and telling everyone so that Jesus could no longer openly enter the city, but stayed in secluded places, and people were coming to Him from everywhere. 35-45

Even after healing late into the night, He is recharged and called to pray in private before anyone else is up. As Peter and friends finally locate Him, they accuse Jesus of wandering off. So Jesus is "interrupted" as He is praying.

So many of His encounters will be "interruptions." Most conversations and miracles are interruptions as He is either teaching or attempting to have solitude. Jesus gives His mission statement: "To go and preach." As He preaches a leper comes to Him. Notice the leper is begging, but also making a statement of faith. "If you are willing, you can make me clean." He knows Jesus has the power and only needs to be willing.

Notice that Jesus not only heals him, but breaks Jewish

law by touching him. In every other instance Jesus would become unclean, yet here the power of Jesus overcomes the leprosy. Surprisingly, Jesus tells him to be silent, a command He will give to many. Yet he spreads the news everywhere. Part of the reason is Jesus is strategic about how He will be revealed, which will be seen after His arrest. Jesus is progressively, on His own time, managing when He would heal. Yet the word is out–He will be pursued by a large crowd for the rest of the gospel.

CHAPTER TWO

Later, having entered again into Capernaum, it was heard that He was in the house, so many gathered that there was no room left, not even at the door, and He taught the word to them. Then four came carrying a paralytic. They were not able to come near him through the crowd. So they removed the roof and having broken it through, they let down the mat he was lying on.

Jesus, seeing their faith, says to the paralytic, "Son, your sins are forgiven." Now some scribes sitting there reasoning in their hearts, "Why does this man speak this, He blasphemes! Who is able to forgive sins but God alone? Immediately, Jesus knowing in His spirit they are reasoning this, says to them. "Why are you reasoning this in your hearts? Which is easier to say to the paralytic, 'Your sins are forgiven' or to say 'Arise and take up your mat and walk'? But, that you may know that the Son of Man has authority to forgive sins on earth.".

He says to the paralytic, "Get up, take your mat

and go home." And he got up and immediately took his mat and left in front of everyone. This amazed everyone and they gave glory to God saying, "We've never seen this." 1-12

Such a bizarre story! There is an enormous crowd present when the four men bring the paralytic to Peter's house. One might think the men might come back later or hang out till the crowd dissipates. Not these guys – one of them has the idea, "We could tear off the roof!?" The audacity to start destroying the home of someone else, which also interrupts Jesus teaching as He is inside speaking and the roof starts caving in. You would expect Jesus to cast these vandals into utter darkness for home invasion. Jesus, instead, sees faith in desperation.

Yet, the story takes another unexpected turn. Jesus forgives the paralytic's sin. A nice gesture, but these guys didn't bring him all this way, over the crowd, and through the roof, to get his sin forgiven. They brought him to be healed. While they might be confused or let down by just being forgiven, the scribes sitting there are silently baffled and outraged. They are the religious teachers who held a stern control over the Jewish people and will challenge Jesus at every turn. They think to themselves that Jesus has blasphemed (religious speech deemed slanderously false.) They make the claim that only God can forgive sins.

Here is the third bizarre turn. The scribes are correct. The scribes and Jesus will have many verbal battles throughout the gospel and they are always wrong, except here. It is true only God can forgive sins. So they accurately recognize the statement Jesus makes in forgiving the man – that Jesus is God. Jesus, reading their minds, confronts them on why they are thinking this way, and then performs the miracle they have all been waiting for – healing the man. Yet, not just for the man's sake. "But that you may know that He has the authority to forgive sins" is the main reveal of the entire story. This is really the first preaching of the gospel: Jesus forgives! Prompted by these four who would literally rip off a roof to get their friend to Jesus.

> *Again He went beside the sea, and the crowd comes to him and he taught them. Going along He sees Levi, the son of Alphaeus, sitting at the tax booth and He says to him, "Follow Me." Getting up, he followed Him.*
>
> *Later he was reclining at Levi's house and many tax collectors and sinners were reclining with Jesus, along with his disciples for there were many who were following Him. When the scribes of the Pharisees saw Him eating with the sinners and tax collectors, they asked His disciples, "Why does He eat with tax collectors and sinners"? Having heard this Jesus says to them, "The healthy have no need of the physician, but the sick. I came not to call the righteous, but sinners." 13-17*

Jesus continues to teach by the lake and decides to choose another disciple. Unexpectedly, He chooses a tax collector to join the four fishermen. He would be considered a traitor to his people as Levi (also called Matthew) would have been expelled from the synagogue, could not be a witness in court, and would be completely disowned by his family.

Rather than trying to hide this new scandalous follower, Jesus goes straight to Levi's house for dinner. The scribes ask why He would associate with such traitors and sinners, Does He not care for His reputation? Jesus, who just demonstrated His power to forgive sins, now joins those who need forgiveness. In Jesus style, He answers the question by another statement of mission: To be the great physician.

> *John's disciples and those of the Pharisees were fasting. They came saying to Him, "Why do John's disciples and the disciples of the Pharisees fast, but Your disciples do not fast?" Jesus said to them, "How can the guests of the groom fast while He is with them? No, as long as He is with them, they do not fast. But, days will come when the groom will be taken from them, and then they will fast."*
>
> *No one sews an unshrunk cloth on old clothing, it will tear away from the patch and make the tear worse. And no one puts new wine into old wineskins. It will burst and the wine and the wineskin is ruined. Instead, put new wine into new wineskins. 21-22*

Fasting was a normal part of Jewish life. Jesus reveals, almost in code, that He will be "taken from them." He is already, in chapter two, speaking of His death, when His followers will fast. He then speaks of His incompatibility with the current system. The old ways will not control Him or His followers. Jesus cannot be added to any existing system. His kingdom will make all others not only obsolete, but the old systems will disallow anyone from entering into the new kingdom of Jesus. This explains why He doesn't go to build followers among the religious or political elite, who must maintain power, but goes among the "blue collar" to build a new kingdom.

> *On the Sabbath, He was passing through the grainfields and His disciples began plucking heads of grain. The Pharisees were saying to Him, "Look, why do they do what is unlawful on the Sabbath?" And He said, "Have you never read what David did when he and those with him were hungry? How he entered the house of God, when Abiathar was high priest, and ate the show-bread which is not lawful to eat except for the priests, and he gave some to those with him?" He said to them, "The Sabbath was made for man, not man for the Sabbath." Therefore the Son of Man is Lord even of the Sabbath. 23-28*

The Pharisees and scribes or some translations "teachers of the law" will continually hound Him. They are always outsmarted by Jesus and lack the authority and power He displays. We keep waiting for them to "get it" and come over to His side. Some Pharisees will become followers, yet most will not. It doesn't matter how amazing Jesus is because they have a specific agenda. They were concerned with specific observances of Jewish law that had become increasingly bloated and designed to control. In particular, laws concerning ceremonial cleanliness, fasting, food laws, the Sabbath, and anything regarding the temple were paramount. No matter what amazing miracle Jesus performs, or how wise His words – so long as He breaks their rules regarding these areas, they will try to destroy Him.

It seems Jesus continually goes out of His way to break these traditions (the new wine bursting their wineskins). Here Jesus highlights the purpose of the law to serve people rather than simply control them. Mark emphasizes that Jesus is Lord of the Sabbath which might not sound like much to modern readers, but to the first century Jew, put Him in the place of divine authority.

CHAPTER THREE

Again He entered the synagogue, and there was a man having a withered hand, and they were watching Him to see if he will heal him on the Sabbath, in order to accuse Him. He says to the man with the withered hand, "Get up here in front of us." He said to them, "Is it lawful to do good on the Sabbath or to do evil, to save life or to kill?" But they were silent.

Looking at them in anger and grieved at their hardness of heart, He says to the man, "Stretch out your hand." He stretched it out and it was completely restored. The Pharisees and Herodians left and immediately plotted how they might destroy Him. 1-6

Again, we have a story involving the breaking of traditional Sabbath laws, which to the religious authority is more important than a man being healed. For many healing stories in Mark, Jesus tells those healed to keep the miracle private because He is revealing Himself strategically. This story is different. Jesus seeks the man out to heal Him on the Sabbath in front of those wanting to accuse Him. He does this to make the statement that it is always the right time to do good and bring life.

Mark also reveals that Jesus is emotionally engaged. He is passionately angered here. The man's healing becomes an object lesson to the opposition and it triggers them to the point of initiating the plot to kill Him. The Pharisees and Herodians, who normally would not be on friendly terms, yet are united in their hatred of Jesus, are already looking for a way to kill Him. Thus only two chapters completed and the crucifixion plot has begun.

> *Jesus withdrew with the disciples to the sea and large crowds from Galilee followed. Hearing all He was doing they came from Judea, Jerusalem, Idumea, and beyond the Jordan, and around Tyre and Sidon. He told the disciples to have a boat waiting for Him on account of the crowd so they would not press on Him. For He had healed many, that those with diseases were pressing upon Him to touch Him. And the evil spirits when they saw Him were falling down before Him and crying out saying, "You are the Son of God!" He strictly ordered them to not make Him known.*
>
> *He goes up on the mountain and calls to Him those He wanted and they went. He appointed twelve, calling them Apostles. He called them to be with Him and that He might send them to preach and have authority to cast out demons. The twelve He appointed are Simon, who He named Peter, James the son of Zebedee and John his brother, He named them Boanerges which is Sons of Thunder, Andrew, Philip, Bartholomew, Matthew, Thomas, James the son of Alphaeus,*

Thaddaeus, Simon the Zealot, and Judas Iscariot who betrayed Him. 7-19

Again, the crowds are an ever present reality from here till the end of the gospel. He has to choose a boat as a stage to keep from being crushed. He is healing diseases and silencing demons. While Jesus has many disciples, these twelve will be Apostles. It is a special designation to represent the twelve tribes of Israel in the Old Testament.

Apostleship was a New Testament office with great authority. When they are listed Peter is always first as the leader, Judas is always listed last and with the reminder that he is the betrayer. Jesus will invest Himself into these twelve, although we do not know much about several of them, every indication is they are anything but the obvious choice for such a mission. He will patiently love and equip His unprofessional crew.

He comes to a house and a crowd comes so they are not even able to eat. When His family heard this, they went to seize Him saying, "He's gone out of his mind." The scribes having come down from Jerusalem were saying, "He is Beelzebul and by the prince of demons He casts out demons."

So He called them, and speaking to them in parables said, "How is Satan to cast out Satan? If a kingdom is divided against itself, it cannot stand, and a house divided against itself cannot stand. And if Satan is rising up against himself he cannot stand, he is coming to an end. No one is able to enter a strong man's house and rob his things, unless he first binds the strong man, then he can rob his house. Truly I tell you, all sins and blasphemies will be forgiven. Yet, whoever shall blaspheme against the Holy Spirit has no forgiveness but is guilty of eternal sin." For they were saying, "He has an evil spirit."

His mother and brothers arrive. Standing outside they sent one to call Him. He was sitting with a crowd around him. They said to him, "Look, your mother and brothers and sister are outside looking for you." He answered, "Who are my mother and brothers?" Looking at those sitting in a circle around him said, "Look, these are my mother and brothers! Whoever shall do the will of God is my brother and sister and mother. 20-35

This is the first section where we see what many call a Markan sandwich. One story starts (the family comes to take Him- bread), then another short story is told (Scribes attribute His power to Satan-the middle), then the first story is concluded (Jesus redefines family- bread). While each story makes a point, there is another point made when we see the whole sandwich.

For the first story, it appears Jesus is not having sufficient meal time due to the crowd. This triggers His mom and siblings to intercede. There is a plot to kill Him, He is hanging out with sinners, and taking on the demonic – but surprisingly it is the meal interruptions that cause a family intervention.

Then scribes coming from Jerusalem, which are the most important ones. They are aware of His power and His ability to win a debate. So they take a new tactic of simply attributing everything He does to Beelzebub, a nickname for

Satan. This might be called the spiritual conspiracy theory, yet Jesus points out the logical absurdity of such a claim. War is not won by self-sabotage. Rather Jesus is tying up the strong man (Satan) so that He can rob His house (driving out Satan's demons). Jesus then says sins and blasphemies (religious speech deemed slanderously false) as forgivable. Yet there is one type of blasphemy that is not forgiven, specifically described as claiming the work of Jesus by the power of the Holy Spirit is the work of demons.

Then His family comes and sends a messenger to send for Him. Jesus uses His questioning technique, "Who are my mother and brothers?" At first one may think His family was correct, He has gone mad for He no longer recognizes them! Yet, he makes a revolutionary statement. His family is composed of those who are with Him doing God's will. We may use the term family loosely for those close to us, yet the Jews defined nearly every aspect of their lives by tribal lineage, which is one reason for the frequent genealogical lists in the Bible.This new definition of family will take root as believers would come to be called the family of God as brothers and sisters doing the will of God the Father.

The point of the sandwich could be that both stories try to lay claim to Jesus' identity. The religious leaders claim His lineage to be Satan and that He is acting out of that spiritual identity. His family lays claim that He should be acting according to His human identity and wish to exercise authority over Him as His earthly family. Jesus will not be subject to either. We are again reminded of the new wine in new wine skins. He will chart His own path as the Father leads Him. The new path includes redefining spiritual family.

CHAPTER FOUR

Again, He began to teach by the sea, the crowd gathered was so large He got into a boat and sat in it on the sea with the crowd on the shore. Teaching many things in parables saying, "Listen, one went out to sow seed, and as he sowed some fell along the road and birds came and ate it. Others fell on rocky places with little soil, it sprang up immediately because the soil was shallow, and the sun rose and scorched it because it had no root and withered away. Others fell among thorns and grew, but thorns choked it so it gave no fruit. Others fell into good soil and began yielding fruit growing and increasing thirty, sixty, and a hundred fold. If you have ears, listen!

And when He was alone, those around Him with the twelve asked Him about this parable. He said, "To you has been given the mystery of the kingdom of God, but to those outside everything is in parable, so that seeing they do not perceive and hearing they do not understand, lest they should turn and be forgiven.

He says to them, "You don't understand this parable? How will you understand any parables? The one sowing, sows the word. These now are the ones along the road, they hear and immediately Satan comes and takes away the word sown in them. Others are the ones sown on rocky ground. They hear the word and immediately receive it with joy. But having no root in themselves, they are temporary, when trouble or persecution arises because of the word they immediately fall away. Others are those sown among thorns, the worries of this life, the deceit of wealth, and the desires for other things come in and choke the word, bearing no fruit. Others are those upon good soil who hear the word and receive it and bring forth fruit thirty, sixty, and a hundred fold. 1-20

A parable is a simple story to reveal Christ's kingdom. It is not only an observation or analogy to be decoded with the intellect. It is a spiritual revelation to be accepted and obeyed by faith and action. Unlike legends or fables we are placed as a character in the parable and it reveals our spiritual wisdom or spiritual blindness.

The disciples are confused by it and Jesus tells them if they don't understand this one, none will make sense. Most parables make a point, but this first one includes God, the truth, evil, temptation, faithfulness, perseverance, money, worry, rewards, etc. It is a microcosm of the entire kingdom. As we shall see, each parable also has an element of shock.

The sower is Christ (and by extension all who would spread His word) giving the same message to all. The first challenge is Satan who by some method robs the word sown directly into the heart, seemingly before there is an opportunity for it to take root. This reveals the spiritual enemy of God and our soul is real. Rather than Satan being characterized as one who makes "bad things happen," Satan's method here is to prevent the truth of God from taking effect. "The Bible is boring. Bible studies aren't my thing..." etc., would be more evidence of the Satanic than what we see in a typical portrayal of Satan in a horror film.

The next scenario is the rocky soil representing a diluted and shallow heart. Just as weeds spring up quickly in the crack of a sidewalk, the immediate "joy" of the word is expressed – all warm and fuzzy. However, inevitably, challenges will come and shallow faith cannot endure. For true faith is deeply rooted and will withstand harsh attack.

Thirdly, is a faith that may appear deeply rooted, but lives a life of entanglement by the world. Believing the truth, yet living for the world. There are three warnings:

1. The worries of this life.
2. The deceitfulness of wealth.
3. The desires for other things.

Rather than suffering for faith, all these are simply the enticements of the world, with the third being all inclusive.

Finally, the good soil. The heart that embraces the good news, allows it to become deeply rooted which allows the plant to not only grow but withstand internal and external challenges. It then bears massive fruit. This is the shock of the parable. On the best year a yield is six fold, but the kingdom is supernatural yielding 30, 60, or even 100. This supernatural yield will be a constant theme in Jesus' teaching on the kingdom.

> *He was saying to them, "A lamp isn't brought under a basket or bed, is it not put on a lampstand? For what is hidden is meant to be made visible, what is secret should be brought to light. If you have ears, listen! Discern what you hear! Whatever measure you use will be measured to you and more added. For whoever has will be given more, and whoever does not have, even what he has will be taken away." 21-25*

Jesus is to reveal the kingdom, it will no longer be hidden and His messengers are called to reveal it. The current religious system of the scribes breeds authoritarianism and hypocrisy, in His kingdom the same measure is applied to all. The "given more" and "taken away" relates to the parable of the soil as well. For one having no faith the seed is taken or withers, while the good soil multiplies exponentially.

> *He was saying, "This is what the kingdom of God is, a man casts seed on the ground and if he sleeps or gets up night and day the seed sprouts and grows, he doesn't know how. The earth brings forth fruit by itself, first a stalk, then the head, then the grain in the head. But when the crop is ready, he immediately sends the sickle for the harvest has come 26-29*

This short parable only occurs in Mark and speaks to the supernatural provision of kingdom growth whereas the faithful sower gets to enjoy a harvest that God has grown.

> *He was saying, "To what shall we compare the kingdom of God? What parable to describe it? As a mustard seed. When sown it is the smallest of all the*

seeds, and when it grows it becomes greater than all the garden plants and makes great branches where birds perch under its shade." With many parables He was speaking the word, as much as they were able to hear. He didn't say anything without parables, but in private with His disciples He would explain everything. 30-34

The mustard seed, the third "sowing" parable in a row, highlights the supernatural growth from a seed that a bird would eat, to a place for birds to perch. So far each teaching has highlighted the supernatural expanse of the kingdom over time for those with faith. The kingdom is not generated by human effort. After His parables the disciples would get an in depth debriefing.

That evening He said, "Let's pass over to the other side." Dismissing the crowd they took Him with them, as He was already in the boat, and there were other boats with Him. A violent wind storm came and the waves were breaking over the boat so that it was filling up. He was in the back of the boat on a cushion asleep.

They woke him saying, "Teacher, don't you care if we die?" Having woken, He rebuked the wind and said to the sea, "Silence, be still!" The wind stopped and all was calm. He said to them, "Why are you fearful – you still have no faith?" They were terrified with great fear and were saying to each other, "Who is this that even the wind and the sea obey Him?" 35-41

Jesus, having taught all day, tells the disciples they are going to the other side of the lake. They now have some rowing to do, for the lake is several miles across to their destination. As Jesus sleeps, a major storm occurs on the sea of Galilee, known for violent storms developing quickly. Several of the disciples being fishermen, have seen their share of storms, yet this one must have been severe. So severe, that the fisherman woke the carpenter not with warning, but with an accusation. "Teacher, Don't you care..." Jesus rebukes the wind then rebukes them for having no faith. They then ask each other about the true identity of Jesus. It is one thing to have the spiritual power to drive out demons or heal, but this cosmic power over nature is new to them. Ironically, their question of Jesus' identity will be answered in the next story.

CHAPTER FIVE

They came to the other side of the sea to the region of the Gerasenes. Just as Jesus left the boat a man met Him from the tombs with an evil spirit. He lived in the tombs and no one could bind him any longer. He often was shackled with chains and had torn the chains to pieces; no one was strong enough to subdue him. All through the night and day in the tombs and the hills he was crying out and cutting himself with stones.

Having seen Jesus from a distance he ran, fell on his knees before Him and crying out loudly said, "What business do we have, Jesus, Son of the most high God! Swear to God you won't torture me!" For He was saying, "Come out of this man you evil spirit." He was asking him, "What is your name?" He answered, "Legion, because we are many." And he begged Him over and over not to send them out of the region.

A herd of pigs were eating near the mountain. They begged Him saying, "Send us into the pigs!" He allowed them, and having gone out of the man into the pigs, the herd rushed down the steep bank into the sea, about 2,000, and were drowned. Those feeding them fled, telling people in the city and country. So people went out to see what happened.

They come to Jesus, and see the man possessed by a legion of demons sitting, dressed, and in his right mind. Those seeing it described what happened to the demon possessed man and the pigs. They began to beg Jesus to leave their region. As Jesus was entering the boat, the man who had been possessed was begging to go with Him. Jesus did not let him, but said, "Go home to your family and tell them how much the Lord has done for you, and how He had mercy on you," He left and began to preach in the Decapolis how much Jesus had done for him and all were amazed. 1-20

Jesus enters this Gentile unclean land with unclean tombs with an unclean man who has an unclean spirit next to unclean pigs. This is the last place a Jewish man would dare enter, yet Jesus is about to reveal His mission is greater than His own Jewish people. As soon as Jesus steps on land the demon possessed man runs to Him.

Remember the disciples just asked during the calming of the storm "Who is this man that the wind and waves obey Him?" Ironically, that question is answered by the demon who gives a theologically correct description, "Jesus, Son of the most high God." This title was given in the first verse of the book and the demon is the first one to correctly identify Jesus. Mark belabors the point that this man is beyond hope, there is no human solution. The demons fear being driven from that region and Jesus honors the request to be driven into pigs which are all quickly drowned. The Gentile pig herders spread the news and people gather.

Just as the demons begged not to leave, the people begged for Jesus to leave. While they may be impressed with the man being healed, they likely equate Jesus' presence as a plague upon their livelihood. The man wants to go with Jesus. He would have a great testimony to share, but Jesus tells him instead to be reunited with his family and to be the first evangelist to the Gentiles who become amazed at the story of Jesus.

> *Jesus passed over by boat to the other side of the sea and a large crowd gathered as He was beside the sea. Jairus, a synagogue ruler, comes and sees Him, and falls at His feet begging Him saying, "My little daughter is barely alive, come lay your hands on her so she might be cured and live." So Jesus went with him.*
>
> *The large crowd was following and pressing in on Him. A woman, bleeding twelve years, had suffered much, had many doctors, and having spent all she had, was no better, but only worse. Having heard about Jesus, she comes up in the crowd behind and touches His clothes. For she was saying, "If I touch just His clothes I will be healed." Immediately her bleeding stopped and she knew in her body that she was free from her suffering.*
>
> *Immediately Jesus, knowing power had gone out from Him, turned in the crowd and said, "Who touched My clothes?" The disciples were saying, "You see this crowd pressing in on you, and you say 'Who touched Me'? He was looking around to see who had done it. The woman, frightened and trembling, knowing*

> *what had happened to her came and fell down before Him and told Him the whole truth. He said to her, "Daughter, your faith has healed you, go in peace, be healed from your affliction."*
>
> *Yet, while He is speaking some come from the house of the synagogue ruler saying. "Your daughter is dead, why trouble the teacher further." Jesus heard them speaking and says to the synagogue ruler, "Do not fear, only believe." He allows no one to follow Him but Peter and James and John the brother of James. They come to the house of the synagogue ruler and he sees a commotion and weeping and wailing. Going in He says to them, "Why all this commotion and weeping? The child is not dead, but sleeping." They were laughing at Him.*
>
> *He then throws them all out and takes with Him the father, and mother, and those with Him and goes to the child. Taking her hand, He says, "Talitha Koum," which translates, "Little girl, get up." Immediately she got up and began walking. She was twelve years old. Immediately, they were overcome with great amazement. He told them strictly that no one should know this and He told them to give her something to eat. 21-43*

Another Markan "sandwich." The story of the bleeding woman sandwiched in between the healing of Jairus's daughter. With no time to rest, Jesus is approached by Jairus. He is a religious leader, one of the few examples of those who believe in Jesus. He pleads with Jesus, knowing He can heal her, otherwise she is on her deathbed. Jesus agrees.

In the massive crowd is a woman who also knows Jesus heals. Without saying anything, she touches Him with faith and Jesus feels the healing power leave Him. An unintended healing!? Jesus could have kept heading to Jairus's house, for this is an emergency, seconds count for the girl to live.

Yet Jesus will not be a "healing dispenser." He wants to connect. He will add a relational encounter to His healing power, which annoys the disciples. How many people have brushed up against them in the crowd? But only one had touched Him in faith. She then tells him the whole truth, like the demonic Jesus just healed, every other human solution had not only failed but left her penniless. Jesus affirms her faith and sends her on her way.

Yet, during this heartwarming encounter, devastating news arrives. People come from Jairus's house saying it is too late, his daughter has died. Jesus tells Jairus to believe and not fear. As they arrive the mourners have already gathered. In those days groups of mourners would be paid to make a commotion as a death announcement for the family. Jesus asks them why all the noise, for the girl is just sleeping.

If anyone else would have said this, it would have been a lie. Yet, Jesus has already planned to raise her and kicks the mourners out of the house to do it privately. Jesus commands to rise and she immediately walks emphasizing total life from death. They are overjoyed beyond description. He prompts them to keep this private, this is a special miracle, the first one to demonstrate power over death. These stories work together highlighting the bold faith of an unclean, unnamed woman similar to the men who tore out the roof to get to Jesus, and the desperate faith of a religious leader who gets to see his daughter live.

CHAPTER SIX

He went out from there and came to His hometown followed by His disciples. On the Sabbath He began to teach in the synagogue, and many hearing Him were shocked, saying, "Where did this man get this stuff, what wisdom has been given Him that He even does miracles by His hands? Isn't this the carpenter, Mary's son, and the brother of James, Joseph, Judas and Simon? Don't His sisters live here with us?" And they were offended by Him.

Jesus said to them, "A prophet has honor except in his hometown, with his relatives, in his own house." He wasn't able to do miracles there, but laid His hands on a few sick people, healing them. And He was amazed because of their unbelief. 1-6

Jesus goes back to Nazareth where He grew up. Rather than being a hometown hero, he is met with envy and disdain. HIs hands should be doing carpentry, not miracles. The phrase "familiarity breeds contempt" comes to mind. He is also referred to as "Mary's son" One would typically be referred to by the name of the father, yet likely an insinuation to Him being thought of as an illegitimate child of Mary who became pregnant before her marriage to Joseph. He has been healing those with faith, here He only heals a few. So far in the ministry of Jesus, people are amazed by Him, now He is the one amazed for He finds no faith among His family and friends.

> *He was going around teaching in the villages and He calls the twelve and began to send them two by two giving them authority over evil spirits and commanding them to take nothing for their journey but a staff – no bread, bag, or money in their belts and to wear sandals and not two shirts.*
>
> *He would say to them, "Wherever you enter a house stay there until you leave that place. Whatever place will not receive you or listen, leave shaking off the dust under your feet as a testimony against them." Going out they preached that people should repent and were casting out many demons, and were anointing many sick people with oil, healing them. 7-13*

Jesus sends them out with interesting instructions. Rather than a packing list, they have an "unpacking list." Almost like survivalists they head out with nothing but the power and calling Jesus gives them. While they have demonstrated little faith and will continue to mess up with petty arguments, etc. This first mission trip is a great success.

> *King Herod heard this for Jesus was well known. Some were saying, "John the Baptist is risen from the dead, this is how He has miraculous powers." Others were saying, "He is Elijah." Now others were saying, "He is a prophet, like the other prophets."*

Hearing this, Herod was saying, "John, whom I beheaded has risen!" For Herod, having seized John and bound him in prison, on account of Herodias, his brother Philip's wife who he married. John had been saying to Herod, "It is not lawful for you to have your brother's wife." Herodias held this against him and wanted to kill him. Yet, she was not able to because Herod was afraid of John knowing him to be a righteous and holy man, so kept him safe.

Herod enjoyed listening to John but was greatly confused by him. An opportunity came when Herod, on his birthday, held a banquet for his nobles, military commanders, and the leading men of Galilee. When the daughter of Herodias came in and danced, it pleased Herod and those with him.

The king said to the girl, "Ask me for whatever you wish and I will give it to you." He swore to her, "Whatever you ask for I will give you up to half my kingdom." Going out she asked her mother, "What shall I ask?" She said, "The head of John the Baptist." Immediately she went to the king saying, "At once, I want you to give to me the head of John the Baptist on a platter."

The king was greatly distressed, yet on account of his oaths and guests would not refuse her. Immediately the king sent an executioner, and commanded his head be brought; he was beheaded in the prison and brought his head on a platter. He gave it to the girl who gave it to her mother. Having heard of this, John's disciples came and put his body in a tomb.

14-29

This is the only story that is not directly focused on the ministry of Jesus. It appears to be placed here to demonstrate the cost of discipleship. Chronologically, it occurred earlier than it appears here. The disciples were just sent out to great ministry success, but the story of John is what they will eventually endure.

This Herod is the son of the Herod who tried to kill Jesus as an infant. As is the case with many biblical leaders, he is evil, abusive, and wields power in a selfish tyrannical fashion. His wife is also his sister-in-law. It's a long story, but John the Baptist was calling it out as sin. Herod has plenty of power but no moral compass or self-control. He is trapped by his words and to keep from further embarrassment commits murder.

> *The Apostles gathered around Jesus and reported to Him all the things they had done and taught. He said to them, "Come by yourselves to a private place and rest a little." For so many were coming and going they couldn't even eat. So they got in the boat to go to the private place. But many saw them leaving and recognized them. People ran to the place by land from the towns and arrived ahead of them.*
>
> *Going out, He saw a great crowd and was moved with compassion for them because they were like sheep without a shepherd. He began to teach them many things. By now it was late, so the disciples came to him saying, "We are in the middle of nowhere, it is already late. Tell them to go to the surrounding villages to buy something to eat." But he answered, "You*

give them something to eat." They said to him, "We should go and spend eight months wages to buy them bread?" He says to them, "How many loaves do you have? Go see." Finding out they said, "Five and two fish." He commanded them to sit in the green grass in groups of hundreds and fifties.

Taking the five loaves and the two fish, looking up to heaven, He blessed and broke the loaves and kept giving it to the disciples to set before the people and He divided the two fish among them all. All ate and were full, and they took up twelve baskets of leftovers of bread and fish. Five thousand men had eaten. 30-44

The disciples can hardly contain their excitement speaking of how much success they have had in ministry. As always, a large crowd comes and they can't even enjoy a meal together. Jesus has the idea for a getaway, a private time of retreat so they can rest and catch up with Jesus. As they get in the boat, the crowd just walks along the shore to their destination. It is almost comical, yet likely quite frustrating for the disciples.

As they get out of the boat the crowd has only grown. Rather than being exasperated, Jesus is filled with compassion and takes on the role of shepherd. It is now late, the disciples have patiently waited all evening for Jesus to finish up with the crowd. They interrupt Him, telling Him to dismiss so they can get food. Jesus's response must have sounded either crazy or insulting.

The miracle of the loaves and fish is more than simply a free lunch for the crowd. It is a miraculous illustration of Jesus teaching the kingdom. Jesus takes what little they have and demonstrates abundance. The parables used seed, here He uses food to make the same kingdom point. In the kingdom God makes abundance. As Jesus will teach later, the baskets of leftovers are a major part of the lesson, just like the 30, 60, or 100 fold harvest of the good soil

> *Immediately, He had the disciples get into the boat and go to the other side to Bethsaida while He dismissed the crowd. After they left, He went to the mountain to pray. As evening had come, they were in the middle of the sea and He was alone on land. Seeing them straining as they row because the wind was against them, just before sunrise He comes to them walking on the sea. He intended to come near them.*
>
> *Having seen Him walking on the sea they thought He was a ghost and cried out. They all saw Him and were terrified. Immediately He spoke to them and says, "Take courage, It is I, do not fear." He went into the boat and the wind stopped. They were exceedingly amazed at this for they did not understand about the loaves, but had hardened hearts. 45-52*

Seems odd at first that Jesus sends the disciples away, but He has more to reveal to them. Jesus prays on the mountain for hours, they are struggling again, not a major storm, but enough to be rowing nowhere. As He walks out on the lake, they assume He is a ghost, but He says "It is I." This is a divine designation of God, the same language used by God as He revealed Himself to Moses at the burning bush.

Interestingly, Mark notes they did not recognize Him because their hearts were hard, they did not understand that with Him there was abundance and peace. The hardness of heart blocks off faith which makes the kingdom impossible to see.

> *They passed over to Gennesaret and anchored. Coming out of the boat they recognized Him and ran around the country and carried the sick on mats to wherever they were hearing he was. Wherever He would go, villages, towns, country, they lay the sick in the marketplaces begging Him that they might touch the fringe of His clothes. All who touched Him were healed. 53-56*

This section summarizes the fame of Jesus and the unlimited grace and healing He brings. He would constantly be pursued and He would continue to heal.

CHAPTER SEVEN

The Pharisees and scribes gathered together from Jerusalem. They had seen some of the disciples were eating with defiled, ceremonially unwashed, hands. The Pharisees and the Jews do not eat unless they wash, holding the tradition of the elders when they come from the marketplace, they do not eat till they have washed, and many other customs they keep like washing of cups, jugs, utensils, and tables.

They asked Him, "Why do Your disciples not walk according to the tradition of the elders, but eat with unwashed hands"? He said to them, "Isaiah was rightly prophesying about you hypocrites, as it is written, 'This people honors me with their lips but their heart is kept far from me.' In vain they worship me with rules of men, having neglected the commandment of God you hold to the traditions of men."

He was saying to them, "You neatly set aside the commands of God to keep your traditions. Moses said, honor your father and mother, and he who speaks evil of them is to be put to death, but you say, If a

> *man says to his father or mother, 'whatever I have that would help you is Corban' (that is a gift to God), you no longer permit him to do anything for his father or mother, nullifying the word of God by your traditions you have handed down. You do many things like that. 1-13*

The religious leaders stress ceremonial cleanliness particularly relating to food laws. This is not a matter of their hands literally being dirty. Mark explains the customs to his reading audience. Then the leaders ask him, or accuse Him, of not having his disciples follow the ceremonial washings.

Jesus makes a hard and fast distinction between their handed down traditions which they have developed over the years versus the actual commands of God as revealed in scripture. He points out with specific examples how they have rejected and even disallowed obedience to the law of Moses by putting their traditions as the supreme priority.

The example Jesus gives is the love and responsibility of caring for one's family. Instead of these relational commands, the Pharisees have invented technicalities of minute detail whereby they would judge everyone else. Jesus is very clear about their hypocrisy. He tells them these errors are not simply missed detail, or even ignorance, but makes their attempts at worshipping God a vanity, lip-service, a sham.

> *Calling the crowd to him, He was saying, "Listen to Me, everyone, and understand. Nothing from outside, going into a man, can make him unclean. But the things coming out of a man make him unclean."*

> *When He entered the house away from the crowd the disciples were asking about the parable. "You still don't understand either. Don't you understand that nothing from outside a man can make him unclean by going into him because it doesn't go into the heart, but the stomach and then out the body?" He made all food clean.*
>
> *He was saying, "Now what comes out of a man is what makes him unclean. From their hearts come evil thoughts, sexual immorality, theft, murder, adulteries, greed, malice, deceit, lewdness, envy, slander, arrogance, and nonsense. All these evils go out from you and make a man unclean. 14-23*

Jesus takes the opportunity to make this a public teachable moment, calling them altogether. He states food doesn't make one unclean. Jesus goes way beyond the argument about ceremonial washings to the very nature of "clean." This is a radical statement and supersedes the Old Testament food laws. So radical that it confuses the disciples who ask Him for clarification.

Jesus responds with what seems obvious to most people today, however to the Jews, their food laws were one of the major observances that set them apart from everyone else. Mark gives us the interpretive statement that Jesus' words make all food clean. In Acts 10 Peter will be forced to eat "unclean food" and it is even then difficult for him.

Jesus then gives an inexhaustible list of what is defiled. It is a list of sins that come from the heart. The list is closely tied to the Ten Commandments. Many include overt actions, not just thoughts. Given Jesus' original criticism is hypocrisy, it makes sense that thoughts and actions would be included in one list, for all these actions begin in the hard heart.

> *From there He went to the region of Tyre. He entered a house, not wanting anyone to know, but He could not stay hidden. Immediately a woman hearing about Him with a little daughter who was possessed by an evil spirit came and fell at His feet. The woman was a Greek Syrophoenician. She kept asking Him to drive the demon out of her daughter. He was saying, "Let the children eat first, for it is not good to take their bread and give it to the dogs." But she answered and says to Him, "Yes, Lord, yet the dogs under the table eat the children's crumbs." "For such a reply, you may go; the demon has left your daughter." Going home, she found the girl lying on the bed and the demon gone. 24-30*

Jesus again is in Gentile territory. He is hiding out, not because He is scared, rather He is teaching His disciples. He is in "unclean" lands again and a woman comes to Him who is also unclean described not only as Greek, but Syrophonecian, highlighting both her ethnic and geographical defilement.

Some have thought His words cruel, calling her a dog. However this is not the case. Jesus, as always, speaks in parables explaining that He would minister to the Jews first. This is partly true, however He has healed the demonic in chapter five who was a Gentile, and is now in Gentile territory.

The woman does something impressive. She enters the parable by faith. Rather than arguing with Jesus or giving up, she affirms what He says is true. Her statement is humble, yet like the men taking off the roof, the bleeding woman, and others, she knows the grace of Jesus is to be pursued boldly. Jesus rewards her for her response and performs the only "distance" exorcism in scripture.

> *Leaving Tyre, he came through Sidon, to the Sea of Galilee, and into the region of the Decapolis. They bring Him a deaf man who can barely speak, and beg Him to lay hands on him. Taking him away from the crowd in private, He put his fingers in the man's ears and He spit and touched the man's tongue. Sighing deeply, He looked to heaven and said to the man, "Ephphatha". That is "Be opened." His ears were opened and immediately his tongue free and he began to speak clearly.*
>
> *He instructed them to tell no one. But as much as He kept telling them, the more they kept speaking about it. They were overwhelmingly amazed saying, "He does all things well, He makes the deaf hear and the mute speak." 31-37*

He leaves one Gentile territory and enters another. We are reminded of Jesus' native language of Aramaic where Mark translates for his Greek speaking audience, "to be opened." Also Jesus tells them to keep this a secret. He has held people to silence several times and will continue to till after His arrest. He has kept the demons quiet so they would not be seen as His spokesperson, and healings are kept quiet so as not to be constantly mobbed. Mark reveals that the more

Jesus tried to operate covertly the more it backfires. The good news cannot be quieted.

CHAPTER EIGHT

In those days, again a large crowd came and not having anything to eat, Jesus calls His disciples to Him and says, "I have compassion on the crowd. They have stayed with Me three days and have nothing to eat. If I send them home hungry, they will faint on the way, for some have come a long way."

And they said to Him, "Where could anyone find enough to feed them in this wilderness?" He says to them, "How many loaves do you have?" They said, "Seven."

He tells the crowd to sit on the ground and taking the seven loaves and giving thanks, He breaks them and keeps giving them to the disciples to set before them, and they serve the crowd. They had a few small fish, and having blessed them He had them also set before the people. All ate and were full, and they took up seven baskets of leftovers. There were about four thousand.

Having sent them away, He got in the boat with the

disciples and went to the region of Dalmanutha. 1-10

It is easily forgotten that Jesus performed two major feeding miracles. Likely this one was in the region of the Decapolis among the Gentiles. It is interesting that Jesus goes to the disciples to state the same problem they brought to Him in the previous feeding. As Jesus poses the problem, the disciples are still in the mindset of spiritual scarcity. So Jesus prompts them by asking the same question as the first miracle concerning what they already have on hand. Again the leftovers (which are way more than what they originally started with) are emphasized. Again, with Jesus there is abundance.

The Pharisees went out and began to argue with Him, demanding a sign from heaven to test Him. Having sighed deeply in His spirit, He says to them, "Why does this generation demand a sign? I tell you the truth, no sign will be given this generation."

Leaving them, He went back to the other side. They forgot to take bread except for one loaf in the boat. He was teaching them saying, "Watch out, be careful of the yeast of the Pharisees and Herod." They were discussing this saying it was because they had no bread.

Knowing this, Jesus says, "Why are you discussing having no bread? You still don't perceive or understand. Are your hearts hard? Do you have eyes but can't see and ears but can't hear? Do you not remember? When I broke the five loaves for the five thousand, how many baskets of leftovers did you pick up?" "Twelve." they said. "And when I broke the seven loaves for the four thousand, how many baskets of

> *left overs did you pick up?" They said, "Seven." He was saying to them, "You still don't understand?" 11-21*

The Pharisees have challenged Jesus' power, the source of His power, His lack of tradition, and now they challenge Him to produce a sign from heaven. Jesus is exasperated and with a deep sigh says "no" and "why." Jesus is calling people to have faith. The demand for a sign is the opposite of faith. He refuses to be manipulated or put on a show for them.

Jesus then warns the disciples about the "yeast" of Pharisees and Herod who represent both religious and political power. Yeast causes exponential growth, and in this case, not good growth. As they gain popularity and power, they are not to become like those who are already abusing that power. Jesus is constantly speaking in parables and again they misunderstand Him by taking Him literally. Even after seeing Jesus do two miracles with an abundance of leftover bread, they are still worried about running out. They still don't "see" the kingdom after two attempts which may explain this next odd miracle?

> *They came to Bethsaida. They bring a blind man to Him and beg Him to touch him. Taking hold of the blind man's hand He led him out of the village and spit on his eyes and laying His hand on him asks him, "Do you see anything?" Looking up, he said, "I see men, but they look like trees walking around." He touched his eyes again and he opened and saw everything clearly. He sent him home saying, "Don't go into the village, or tell anyone." 22-26*

This fascinating miracle only occurs in Mark. As with other miracles, it is not simply a supernatural act, but an illustration of His teaching. How could Jesus, who has calmed two storms, performed exorcisms from a distance, and who just raised a girl from the dead, not be able to cure blindness in one attempt?

One possible explanation is this miracle follows the second miraculous feeding. Jesus fed the 5,000 with leftovers and the disciples' hearts were still hard, he fed 4,000 with leftovers and they immediately are concerned with having no bread. Two miracles for the disciples to "see" that with Jesus there is an abundant kingdom, yet they still don't see clearly. Thus this healing could be a commentary on how hard it is for His followers to see. Again, Jesus keeps His miracle quiet and away from the crowd. The time has not come for Him to reveal in full.

> *Jesus and the disciples went to the villages of Caesarea Phillipi. On the way Jesus was asking them, "Who do men say I am?" They answered, "John the Baptist, and others say Elijah, and others one of the prophets." Questioning them further, "What about you? Who do you say I am?" Peter, answering Him, says, "You are the Christ." They warned them not to tell anyone about Him.*
>
> *And He began to teach them that the Son of Man must be rejected and suffer many things by the elders, chief priests, and scribes and must be killed, and after three days rise. He spoke bluntly about it. Peter took Him aside and began to admonish Him. Having turned and looking at His disciples, He rebuked Peter*

saying, "Get behind me Satan, you do not have in mind the things of God, but the things of men." 27-33

At first it may sound like Jesus is catching up on the latest gossip about Himself. Yet, He is probing the disciples to see if they are still thinking like the crowd. Peter makes the great confession and at this point the gospel will shift from miracles and speaking of faith to suffering and the cost of discipleship.

Jesus again invokes their silence. He has revealed His complete identity to them. They know He is the messiah, but they do not know what the messiah must do, thus Peter is trying to take over. While Peter's intention and boldness may be admired, it is a way opposite the calling of Jesus. They want the messiah to be an earthly king. Jesus will be king, but must first be a sacrificial savior.

Having called the crowd with His disciples he said, "If anyone desires to follow Me, let him come and deny himself and take up his cross and follow Me. For whoever desires to save his life will lose it. Whoever will lose his life on account of Me and the gospel will save it.

What good does it do for a man to gain the whole world and lose His soul? What will he give in exchange for his soul? Whoever is ashamed of Me and My words in this adulterous and sinful generation, so the Son of Man will be ashamed of him when He comes in His Father's glory with the holy angels." He was saying to them, "Truly I say to you there are some standing here who will not taste death before they see the kingdom of God come with power." 31-9:1

In the first half of Mark, Jesus has demonstrated His authority and defined true faith in His kingdom. Jesus now illustrates the stakes of discipleship in His kingdom. So far, with His teachings and miracles people have been constantly "amazed." However, being amazed is not the same as being a disciple.

This is the first mention of the word "cross." The cross is the only way to be a follower. If these words were in the first chapter, people would think Him an egomaniac. Yet, now that the crucifixion is near, now that He has demonstrated His power, He demands allegiance from His followers. Any other way of life, even to gain the whole world is a tragic loss. This is also a foreshadowing of His return in the Father's glory. Yet, Jesus is not finished with His mission on earth and Peter, James, and John are about to see the kingdom come with power.

CHAPTER NINE

After six days Jesus takes Peter, James, and John and brings them up a high mountain alone. There He was transfigured before them. His clothes became more radiantly white than anyone could ever bleach them. Elijah and Moses appeared to them and were talking with Jesus. Peter says, "Teacher, it is good to be here, let us build three tents, one for You, one for Moses, and one for Elijah." They were so terrified they did not know what to say. There came a cloud overshadowing them. A voice came out of the cloud, "This is My son I love. Listen to Him."

Suddenly, looking around they saw no one except Jesus with them. Going down the mountain He instructed them to tell no one what they had seen until the Son of Man had risen from the dead. They kept the matter to themselves questioning what it means to rise from the dead. And they were asking Him, saying, "The scribes say Elijah must come first." And He says, "Sure, Elijah comes first and restores all things. Yet how has it been written about the Son of Man that He must suffer many things and be despised? But

I say to you Elijah has come first and they have done to Him everything they wished, just as it is written about him." 2-13

The Mount of Transfiguration could also be translated as "transformation." It is an otherworldly scene. The three disciples get a glimpse of the spiritual realm, it is so impressive that Peter would like to make camp. Similar to the baptism, the voice of the father breaks through, "This is My son I love, Listen to Him."

While so much heavenly mystery is occurring, these words of the Father are clear. Jesus just defined sacrificial discipleship and the Father tells us to listen. Jesus tells them to keep quiet until after the resurrection. So far they do not understand the crucifixion so they have no idea what the resurrection entails.

Moses and Elijah may represent the law and the prophets and while Moses is the more central figure in the Old Testament, the disciples ask about Elijah. They now know He is the messiah, yet the last words of the Old Testament in Malachi 4, God says He will send the prophet Elijah before the day of the Lord. So the religious leaders were always on the lookout for the return of Elijah. Jesus explains that Elijah has come, not the Elijah they just saw on the mountain, but John the Baptist is the Elijah. Jesus reveals that the religious and political leaders treated John the same way they will soon treat Him.

Coming to the disciples, they saw a great crowd around them and scribes arguing with them. Immediately the crowd seeing Jesus were utterly amazed and ran to greet Him. He asked them, "What is your ar-

gument with them?" One from the crowd answered, "Teacher, I brought my son to you having a mute spirit. When it seizes him, it throws him down and he foams at the mouth, and is withering away. I spoke to your disciples that they might cast it out, but they could not."

He says, "O unbelieving generation, how long will I be with you, how long to endure with you? Bring him to Me." They brought him, and the spirit seeing Him immediately threw him into convulsions, and falling on the ground, began rolling around, and foaming at the mouth. He asked his father, "How long has it been in him?" He said, "From childhood, it often throws him into fire and water to kill him. But if there's anything you can do, help us have pity on us."

Jesus said to him, "If you are able? All things are possible to the one believing." Immediately the father cried out, "I believe, help my unbelief." Jesus seeing the crowd running together, He rebuked the evil spirit saying, "mute and deaf spirit I command you to come out of him and never enter again." The spirit crying out threw him into convulsions and came out. He looked dead. Many said he was dead. But Jesus taking him by the hand lifted him and he arose.

Having entered the house the disciples asked privately, "Why were we not able to cast it out?" He said to them, "This kind can only come out by prayer." 14-29

The story transitions from a mountain top transformation, to arguments and demons afflicting children in a matter of moments. As soon as Jesus is trying to intercede, a man shouts out the horrible testimony of what his family has endured. Even the disciples couldn't help. The father, with a desperate plea, addresses Jesus with "if you can help."

Of all the commotion, crowd, arguing, demons, Jesus focuses on that one word "if." Then reveals one of the most famous verses concerning faith and all things being possible. We see the context of this verse is not a soft message of sweet inspiration, but a spiritual battle cry of desperation. The father responds with a spiritually honest confession. Claiming at once that he does believe and also that he struggles with unbelief.

With all the religious hype and lack of faith Jesus encounters, this statement is unique. As the demon in the child sees Jesus, it throws him into convulsions. Jesus asks how long this has been going on and the answer tells us this is no recent condition. This demon wanted to kill his son one way or another, thus the father's desperation and challenge of faith is understandable. As always, the crowd is on His heels, so He drives out the demon causing such convulsion that he appears dead.

Later, the disciples who have driven out demons when they went out two by two in chapter six wonder why they could not drive out this one. It appears whatever method they had used would not dislodge this demon that had such a hold on the boy, perhaps they had tried everything except prayer?

> *From there they were passing through Galilee and He didn't want anyone to know for He was teaching the disciples and he was saying, The son of Man is de-*

livered into the hands of men and they will kill Him, and having been killed on the third day He will rise. Yet they did not understand and they were afraid to ask Him.

And they came to Capernaum, and in the house He was asking them, "What were you discussing on the way here?" They kept quiet, for they had been discussing which was the greatest. Sitting down, He called the twelve and says to them, "If anyone desires to be first, he will be last and servant of all." Setting a child among them and having taken it in His arms, He said to them, "Whoever shall receive little children in My name, receives Me and not just Me but the one sending Me." 30-37

Jesus again shares the secret of His mission with the disciples, each time with more detail. Yet, as has been the pattern, they misunderstand Him. Typically Jesus is speaking figuratively and they misunderstand Him by taking Him literally. Now He speaks of the crucifixion and resurrection literally and they perhaps think He is being figurative? Either way they are scared to ask Him about it.

It could have been a fear that if they did understand, they would not be able to bear it. However as they reach Capernaum, Jesus asks them about the argument along the way. It is revealing. The inner circle of James, John, and Peter have just witnessed the transfiguration, saw Moses and Elijah, and heard the voice of the Father, while the other nine combined couldn't drive a demon out of a boy.

Perhaps egos and defensiveness were soaring, even as Jesus was speaking about His impending death. A child becomes

His visual aid for the humility they are to exhibit. To show hospitality and to defer to a child who has nothing to give in return is a sign of greatness in His kingdom. To welcome one who deserves nothing is to welcome both the Father and the Son.

John answered him, "Teacher we saw someone casting out demons in your name, who does not follow us. We stopped him because he was not following us."

Do not stop him, no one doing a miracle in My name is able to speak evil of Me. For whoever is not against us is for us. Whoever gives a cup of water in my name because you are Christ's, will certainly not lose his reward. And whoever causes one of the little ones believing in me to stumble, it is better for him to put a heavy millstone around his neck and be cast into the sea.

If your hand causes you to sin, cut it off. It is better for you to enter into life crippled than with two hands going into hell in unquenchable fire. If your foot causes you to sin, cut it off. It is better for you to enter into life lame than with two feet and be cast into hell. And if your eye causes you to sin, cast it out. It is better for you to enter the kingdom of God with one eye than with two eyes and be cast into hell where their worm never dies and the fire is not quenched.

Everyone will be seasoned with fire. And every sacrifice is seasoned with salt. Salt is good. However, if salt becomes unsalty with what will you season it? Have salt in yourselves and be at peace with one another." 38-50

Along with the lack of prayer and narcissistic arguing, John now adds discrimination against others who are doing the will of Jesus but happen to not be in the immediate Apostleship. Obviously John thinks he is doing the right thing or he wouldn't be telling Jesus about it with such confidence. Jesus uses this teachable moment to say even such an act as a cup of water is rewarded. His kingdom will not be one of status and partiality.

He then turns His attention to the child and with very clear and harsh language speaks protection over them. Similar to the recent statement of "gaining the world and losing your soul" yet here causing the little one to sin is also grounds for losing the soul.

The "worm and fire" is a quote from Isaiah speaking of the eternal nature of punishment. The salt is required for all sacrifice and must remain pure or it loses its flavor. Jesus ends His talk with, "Be at Peace with each other." This refers to the arguing and the others outside their group who are following Jesus.

CHAPTER TEN

Going up from there He comes into the region of Judea and beyond the Jordan and crowds come to Him and as usual He was teaching them. Testing Him, The Pharisees interrogated him, "Is it lawful for a husband to divorce his wife?"

He answered, said to them "What did Moses command you?" "Moses allowed to write divorce papers and to send her away." But Jesus said to them, "Because of your hardness of heart, he wrote that commandment for you. However from the beginning of creation, He made them male and female. On account of this, a man will leave his father and mother and be joined to his wife and the two will be one flesh. Therefore no longer are they two but one flesh. Therefore what God has joined together let man not separate.

Entering the house again, the disciples asked Him about this. And he said to them, "Whoever divorces his wife and marries another commits adultery against her. And if a woman divorces her husband

and marries another, she commits adultery. 1-12

While Jesus is the great model of forgiveness and eats with tax collectors and sinners, when it comes to marriage and divorce, He takes the most extremely conservative position. It was one of the most controversial issues of the day and they were hoping to divide His followers over His answer. He appeals to Moses, who did allow divorce. Then, He claims that law was not the intention, but existed because of their hardness of heart. He then goes back to the created design for marriage. Jesus' position is so strict that the disciples have to clarify which He does. Preserving marriage was, and remains, one of the clearest commands of Jesus.

> *And they were bringing little children to him, that He might touch them, but the disciples admonished them. Seeing this, Jesus was angry and said to them. Let the little children come to me, do not forbid them. For the kingdom of God belongs to such as these. Truly I say to you, whoever shall not receive the kingdom of God as a child shall never enter it. Taking them in His arms He laid his hands on them, blessing them.* 13-16

Interesting that children immediately enter the narrative following the divorce statement. For they are so often its primary victims. Jesus is angry. He was just holding a child in his arms as a warning that it is better to drown than to mislead a child. Then Jesus makes a statement more extreme than the divorce statement. The kingdom belongs to them, more than that they are the model of entering the kingdom. So far the kingdom has been compared in parables to sowers, seeds, and many other things, but the only human example of the kingdom is the child. Jesus doesn't simply stop with theory, but takes the children in His arms and blesses them.

> *Going along the road, one running up and kneeling down to Him asked Him, "Good teacher, What shall I do to inherit eternal life?" Jesus said to him, "Why do you call me good? None is good but God alone. You know the commandments, Do not murder, do not commit adultery, do not steal, do not bear false witness, do not defraud, honor your father and mother. And he was saying to Him, "Teacher, all these I have kept since I was young."*
>
> *Jesus looking at him, loved him and said, "One thing you're lacking. Go, sell what you have and give to the poor, and you will have treasure in heaven and come follow me." Hearing this, he was shocked, and went away in grief, for he had a lot of stuff. 17-22*

Finally, someone comes and asks the most important question, eternal life. He is focused, direct, wealthy, young, and moral. Jesus starts listing the commands and the man has apparently lived them. Jesus loves him. He wants him as a follower.

It appears the young man has everything. Ironically, Jesus points out that he is lacking. Even more ironic, what he is lacking is that he has never lacked. Jesus sets the terms of discipleship and the man is shocked. Jesus just taught one must be dependent like a child, this man was apparently dependent upon himself. He leaves saddened. He is spiritually minded enough to know he should follow Jesus, but not spiritual enough to deny himself. He becomes an example of the seed sown among thorns in chapter four, "the deceit of wealth" that chokes the word.

> *Looking around, Jesus said to the disciples, "How hard it is for those with wealth to enter the kingdom of God." The disciples were amazed at His words. But Jesus again says to them, "Children, how hard it is for those who trust in riches to enter the kingdom of God. It is easier for a camel to go through the eye of the needle, than for a rich man to enter the kingdom of God." They were absolutely amazed, saying, "Then who can be saved?"*
>
> *Looking at them, Jesus says, "It is impossible, with man, but not with God, for all things are possible with God." Peter began saying to Him, "Look, we left everything and followed you."*
>
> *Jesus says to them, Truly, I tell you no one who has left home, brothers, sisters, mother, father, children, or lands, for My sake and for the gospel, shall take a hundredfold in this time, houses, brothers, sisters, mothers, children, lands, with persecutions, and in the coming age eternal life. However, many first will be last and the last first. 23-31*

The disciples are also shocked at Jesus' statement about the wealthy entering the kingdom of God. They were likely thinking Jesus missed an opportunity to add a young man with such a resume and resource to their group. They cannot believe that such worldly status would be a hindrance, so much so, they ask, "Who then can be saved?"

Jesus answers again with a famous often quoted truth. "It is impossible with man, but not with God, all things are possible with God." If it would have been possible for man to save himself, this would have been the man capable.

Jesus is teaching that salvation is only from God. The Apostles want to make sure they are in good standing. Jesus affirms those who have chosen God over the world will receive their reward with part of that reward being persecutions for the faith. He concludes with the first and last switching places to sum up that His kingdom is upside down from the world as illustrated by the man who is first in world, but last in the kingdom.

> *They were going up the way to Jerusalem and Jesus was leading with followers amazed and afraid. Taking the twelve aside again, He began telling them what was going to happen to Him. "Look, we will go up to Jerusalem and the son of man will be betrayed to the chief priests and the scribes. They will condemn Him to death and will betray Him to the Gentiles. They will mock Him, spit on Him, flog Him, and kill Him, and on the third day He will rise again."*

> *The two sons of Zebedee, James and John, come up to Him saying, "Teacher, we want You to do whatever we ask." "What do you want Me to do for you?" They said to Him, "Grant to us that one may be at Your right hand and the other at Your left hand, that we might sit in Your glory." Jesus said to them, "You don't know what you ask. Are you able to drink the cup I drink and be baptized in the way I will?" And they said to Him, "We are able." Jesus said to them, "The cup I drink, you will drink. You will be baptized as I will, but to sit at My right hand or left hand is not*

> *Mine to give, but given to those for whom it has been prepared."*
>
> *Hearing this the ten began to be incensed at James and John. Calling them close, Jesus says to them, "You know how the Gentile rulers exercise lordship, how their great ones dominate authority over them. This is not how it will be among you. Instead, whoever desires to become great will be your servant, and whoever desires to be first will be slave of all. Even the Son of Man came not to be served, but to serve and to give His life as a ransom for many." 32-45*

Jesus gives His third prediction of His upcoming death in greater detail. Now the Gentiles are involved, meaning the political authorities. It reads as if James and John come with their request immediately after this announcement. Everyone knew Peter, James, and John were the inner circle, and Peter was just knocked down a notch by Jesus referring to him as "Satan." So James and John hope to secure their spot. While they did not know what it meant to be at His right and left, they assumed it meant "glory." Jesus informs them that suffering is what they will endure and the Father has prepared such spaces.

News travels to the ten and they feel betrayed, or perhaps slow since they didn't think to secure their spots first. Jesus then teaches the clash of kingdoms, saying they are acting like the world. They are fighting for power rather than His kingdom of service. To be "first is to be slave of all" sounds as ridiculous to them as it does to the way our world works today. Then what may be the theme verse of the gospel. Jesus being the ultimate servant who will give His life as payment for the sins of the world.

> *They come to Jericho and as they are leaving Jericho with the disciples and a large crowd, the son of Timaeus, Bartimaeus, a blind beggar, was sitting beside the road. Having heard it was Jesus of Nazareth, he began to cry out and say, "Son of David, Jesus, have mercy on me." And they were rebuking him that he would shut up, but he kept crying out more, "Son of David, have mercy on me."*
>
> *Jesus stopped and told them to call him and they called for him saying "Take courage! Get up! He calls you!" And throwing off his cloak, he rose and came to Jesus. Jesus says, "What do you want me to do for you?" The blind man said to Him, "Teacher, that I can see." Jesus said, "Go, your faith has healed you." Immediately he received sight and he began following Him on the road." 46-52*

Bartimaeus, like the children, and so many others who have come to Him, is helpless and can only receive grace from Jesus. He is a forgotten outsider who Jesus hears. Jesus heals him instantly. This is the last healing miracle and it mirrors the first of Peter's mother in law. A healing, followed by the one healed serving and following. Now Bartimaeus is literally a follower as he joins the disciples on the road to Jerusalem.

CHAPTER ELEVEN

As they drew near Jerusalem, at Bethpage and Bethany near the Mount of Olives, He sends two disciples and says, "Go into the village ahead of you, and immediately you will find a colt tied that no one has ever sat upon. Untie it and bring it. If anyone says to you, 'Why are you doing this?' Say, "The Lord needs it and will return it here soon.'" They left and found the colt tied at a door outside by the street and they untied it. Some of those standing there were saying, "What are you doing untying the colt?" They spoke to them as Jesus commanded and they allowed them.

They led the colt to Jesus and put their cloaks on it and He sat on it. Many spread their cloaks on the road, others branches they cut from the fields. Those going before and those following were crying out, "Hosanna! Blessed is the one coming in the name of the Lord! Blessed is the coming kingdom of our father David! Hosanna in the highest!"

He entered Jerusalem and into the temple. After having looked around at everything, since it was already late, He went out to Bethany with the twelve. 1-11

Here, there is plenty of detail about Jesus' ride into town. Rather than a royal stead, He will ride a humble donkey (a borrowed one at that) to fulfill the prophecy of Zechariah 9:9.

All the excitement is not specifically for Jesus although He does get positive attention. This is Preparation for the Passover, thousands of people are rushing into the city singing Psalms of "Hosanna" (Psalm 118). For the moment, He is like a grand marshal of the Passover parade. Just as quickly as the crowd cheers Him, they will soon turn on Him. Plenty of hype, but no faith. He will not be the messiah they will be looking to embrace. He arrives in Jerusalem, does a quick tour and leaves.

The next day, leaving Bethany, He was hungry. Seeing a fig tree in the distance, He went to it, but he found nothing but leaves, for it was not the season for figs. He says, "No one will ever eat fruit from you!" And the disciples heard Him.

They come into Jerusalem and entering the temple, he began to cast out those selling and buying. He overturned the tables of the money changers and the seats of those selling doves. And he would not allow anyone to carry things through the temple. He was teaching, saying "Is it not written, My house will be called a house of prayer for all nations, however you have made it a den of thieves!" The chief priests and scribes heard it and they were looking how to destroy Him for they were afraid of Him, for all the crowd was amazed at His teaching. When evening came they left the city.

Passing by the next morning they saw the fig tree dried up from the roots. Remembering, Peter says to Him, "Teacher, look the fig tree You cursed is withered." Jesus answering says to them, "Have faith in God. Truly I tell you whoever shall say to this mountain, 'Be cast into the sea' and does not doubt but believes in his heart what he says will take place, it will be done for him. Because of this, I say to you, all things you pray for, believe you have received it, and it will be given. When you stand praying, forgive anything you have against anyone so that also your father in heaven may forgive your trespasses." 12-25

Possibly another sandwich. The Fig tree encounters on both sides with the cleansing of the temple in the middle. Symbolically, Israel is a fig tree (Jeremiah 8) that is to bear fruit. Yet, it has become a barren religion. The cursing of the tree becomes an "action parable" for the cursing He performs in the temple. It has become a "den of thieves" meaning not just where mistakes are made, but a "hideout" where all corruption is openly sanctioned. This action scares the leaders of the corruption, and the plot to kill him accelerates.

The next day, Peter points out the withered tree. Jesus' response is to have faith in God, an odd response to a dead tree. Yet, Jesus reemphasizes kingdom faith, the same faith He has been teaching all along as the only cure for the root rot that plagues the world. This kingdom faith is bold, from the heart, and forgiving.

They come again to Jerusalem and as He is walking in

> *the temple, the chief priests, scribes, and elders come to Him and say, "By what authority are you doing these things?" or "Who gave you the authority to do these things?" Jesus said to them, "I will ask you one question, you answer Me, and I will tell you by what authority I do these things. The baptism of John, was it from heaven or from men? Answer Me."*
>
> *They began discussing among themselves saying, "If we say from heaven, He will say, 'Why did you not believe him?' But if we say 'From men?' They were afraid of the people for everyone held that John truly was a prophet, so they answered Jesus saying, "We do not know." Jesus says to them, "Neither will I tell you by what authority I do these things." 27-33*

In such a corrupt system, only corruption will rise to the top. Those leading the corruption come to question His authority. Jesus responds with a question which reveals they are not legitimate authority but are only people pleasers. They are not interested in truth, so Jesus will not continue to reveal anything to them. He will reveal His authority to them after He is arrested.

CHAPTER TWELVE

And He began to speak to them in parables. "A man planted a vineyard, and placed a fence around it, dug a wine vat, and built a tower, and rented it to workers and traveled abroad. At harvest time he sent a servant to the workers to receive some of the fruit of the vineyard. But they took him and beat him and sent him away with nothing.

He sent them another servant. They hit him on the head and insulted him. He sent another, and they killed him. He sent many others, they were beating some and killing others. Now having one left, his son whom he loved, he sent him last saying, "They will revere my son." Yet the workers said to themselves, 'Look, this is the heir. Come let's kill him and the inheritance will be ours.' Taking him, they killed him, and threw him out of the vineyard.

What will the owner of the vineyard do? He will kill those workers and give the vineyard to others. Have you not read the scripture, 'The stone rejected by the builders has become the capstone. The Lord has done this and it is marvelous in our eyes'".

They were looking to lay hold of Him, but they feared the crowd, for they knew He had spoken the parable against them, so they left and went away. 1-12

Jesus retells a parable from Isaiah 5. Isaiah was speaking of all of Israel, whereas Jesus uses it for the religious leaders of Israel. Also, in Isaiah's parable the vineyard is destroyed, Jesus says this vineyard will be given to others. It will be given to His new kingdom followers who will bear fruit. The servants represent the prophets who they have ignored, beat, or killed.

As with most parables, there is an element of shock. Why would the owner, after such treachery, send his only son to such violent assailants? It is another prediction of His crucifixion. The parable displays the level of evil it takes for it to happen. Workers, who should be stewards, are emboldened to act as brutal owners who think they can get away with killing the owner's son.

He then quotes that He is the stone that is the most important who has been rejected (Psalm 118). Even in their evil plotting the Lord superintends the ultimate plan for His Son to meet a savage death. While Jesus is direct enough, and the leaders are smart enough to see He is targeting them, the only thing more powerful than their hatred for Him is their fear of the crowd-they back down for now.

And they sent some Pharisees and Herodians to Him to ensnare Him in His words. They come and say to Him, "Teacher, we know You are truthful. You defer to no one, or care about appearances, but teach the true way of God. Is it lawful to pay taxes to Caesar or not, should we pay or shouldn't we?" And knowing their hypocrisy, He said to them, "Why do you try to trap me? Bring me a Denarius to see." They brought it and He said to them, "Whose likeness and inscription is this?" They said, "Caesar's." Jesus said to them, "Give to Caesar what is Caesar's, and the things of God back to God." And they were amazed at Him. 13-17

Again, they come with different tactics to take Him down. They hope to trap Him by saying the wrong thing on a very sensitive issue which may turn half the crowd against Him. The smear campaign starts with flattery, to have Him drop His guard, before they go in for the kill. Taxes are as controversial then as they are today. Yet, Jesus flips the argument to allegiance. He asks for a denarius which has a picture of Caesar with the inscription above the image reading "divine son of Augustus." The other side reads, "high priest." The coin is created in Caesar's image, give it back to him. Yet, we are created in God's image, give yourself to Him. Rather than being tripped up with a tax question, Jesus creates a powerful lesson on discipleship.

The Sadducees who say there is no resurrection come to him and question Him saying, "Teacher, Moses wrote for us that if a brother should die and leave behind a wife and no children, that his brother should take the wife and raise up children for his brother. There were seven brothers. The first took a wife and died leaving no children. The second brother took her and died leaving no children and likewise the third. All seven died leaving no children. Last of all the woman died. In the resurrection, when they rise, whose wife will she be? For all seven had her as a wife?"

Jesus was saying to them, "Are you not wrong because you do not know the scripture or the power of God? When the dead rise they neither marry nor are given in marriage, but are like angels in heaven. Now, concerning the dead rising, have you not read in the book of Moses, concerning the Bush, how God spoke to him saying, 'I am the God of Abraham, and the God of Isaac, and the God of Jacob. He is not the God of the dead, but of the living, You are badly mistaken."
18-27

The Sadducees, who are the intellectually liberal elite, and only believe in the first five books of the Old Testament (books of Moses), now try to trap Him with a riddle about the resurrection. Most of what we read about a resurrection comes after the books of Moses. Yet Jesus will beat them using their own book and revealing to them that they do not even know these scriptures, nor do they know the power of God. Whatever we will be in the resurrection supersedes marriage and taking it a step further, Jesus reveals that the Father introducing Himself to Moses at the burning bush is evidence of the afterlife and resurrection, by simply the verb tense "is" rather than "was."

Then one of the scribes come up, having heard them discussing, and seeing that He answered them well, asked Him, "Which is the most important commandment?" Jesus answered, "The most important is, Hear O Israel, the Lord our God, the Lord is One. And you shall love the Lord your God with all your heart and with all your soul and with all your mind, and with all your strength. The second is this. You shall love your neighbor as yourself. There is no greater commandment than these."

The scribe said to Him, "Right Teacher. You have spoken the truth that He is One and there is no other besides Him, and to love Him with all your heart and with all your understanding and with all your strength and to love your neighbor as oneself is more important than all the burnt offerings and sacrifices." And Jesus, seeing him answer wisely, said to him, "You are not far from the kingdom of God." And no one dared ask him more questions. 28-34

The scribes have been His enemies, but this one seems to at least be neutral and asks Jesus a very important question. So much of the discussion among the religious teachers concerned ranking the commandments. Jesus responds with declaring who God is and how we are to give our whole selves to Him and to treat others the same. These may be found in the Old Testament (Deuteronomy 6:4, Leviticus 19:8) but were ignored. This scribe agrees and sums up Jesus' words.

For that response, Jesus gives one of the greatest compliments – the kingdom is within reach for him. Jesus has taken on every opponent from every angle and has been so victorious that no one will dare ask Him another question. At this point it looks like He has won, but His mission is not to win arguments, He will still give His life as a ransom for many.

As Jesus was teaching in the temple He was saying,

"How do the scribes say that the Christ is the son of David?" David, Himself, said by the Holy Spirit, 'The Lord said to my Lord. Sit at my right hand until I place your enemies under your feet.' David, Himself, calls Him Lord, how then is He his son?'" And the great crowd listened gladly to him. 35-37

The teaching of the scribes was that the messiah would be a descendant of David, a man who would reign as an earthly king who would bring Israel back to its military and economic power. Jesus quotes Psalm 110 to demonstrate the messiah will not just be a man but will be a divine Lord.

In His teaching, He was saying, Beware of the scribes loving to walk about in fancy robes, and to be greeted in the marketplaces, and the best seats in the synagogues and at the feasts. They devour widow's houses and show off with long prayers. They will receive greater judgement." 38-40

Going on the offensive, Jesus warns the crowd of the hypocrisy as the leaders use religion to control others and to enjoy the spoils of privilege. They want to be honored by others and are living off the generosity of widows with long prayers to show off. They are enjoying ill-gotten rewards now, but will receive judgement in the future.

Having sat down opposite the treasury, He was watching how the crowd put money into the treasury. Many rich people were putting in much, and one poor widow comes and puts in two small coins worth hardly anything. Calling the disciples to Him, He says, "I tell you the truth, this poor widow put in more than the rest into the treasury. For they all gave out of

> *their excess, however, she gave out of her poverty, all she had to live on."* 41-44

Perhaps this was one of the widows the religious leaders have been manipulating? She gave everything, and in Jesus' kingdom where loving with everything, giving heart, soul, mind, strength, she is the picture of sacrificial discipleship. She serves the opposite example of the rich young man who was shocked that Jesus asked him to sell his stuff. Ironically, the temple treasury was partly to help the poor and she puts in everything.

CHAPTER THIRTEEN

He leaves the temple, and one of the disciples says to Him, "Teacher, Look what stones and buildings!" Jesus said to him, "You see these great buildings? No, not one stone will be left on another, all will be thrown down."

Sitting upon the Mount of Olives, opposite the temple, Peter, James, John, and Andrew asked Him in private, "Tell us when these things will be? What will be the sign when these things will all be fulfilled?" Jesus began saying to them, "Look, let no one mislead you. Many will come in my name saying I am He and mislead many. When you hear of wars and rumors of wars, do not be alarmed, it must come to pass but the end is yet to come. Nation will rise up against nation and kingdom against kingdom. There will be earthquakes in different places, and famines. These are the beginning of birth pains.1-8

This longest monologue of Jesus is daunting. It begins with Jesus casting judgment on this great temple being destroyed which would happen in 70

AD, the four disciples want more detail. Rather than Jesus giving precise signs they ask for, Jesus warns against putting trust in false teachers and cites many examples of what are *not* signs. Even amid great catastrophe, do not assume it is the end.

> *Be on your guard, They will betray you to the councils and you will be beaten in the synagogues. Because of me you will stand before governors and kings to give testimony. The gospel first must be preached to all nations. And when they lead you to trial and arrest you, do not be anxious beforehand about what you should say, but say whatever is given you in that hour. For it will not be you speaking, but the Holy Spirit.*
>
> *Brother will betray brother to death, and a father his child, children will rise up against parents and will put them to death. You will be hated by all on account of me. However the one enduring to the end will be saved. 9-13*

This is still focusing on the cost of discipleship which becomes high as the world increasingly comes after them. They will be put in extraordinary situations when all they have is their faith. That is when their faith and the power of the Holy Spirit will prevail. All earthly relationships will break down. They must stand firm in faith as the world comes against them..

> *When you see the abomination of desolation, standing where it should not, reader understand, then those in Judea flee to the mountains, and the one on his house not come down to go in to take anything out. The one in the field should not return to get his*

coat. How awful for pregnant women and nursing mothers in those days. Pray that does not happen in winter. It will be days of tribulation that have never been seen from the beginning of creation, when God created, until now and never to be again.

If the Lord had not shortened those days no one would be saved, but on account of the elect whom He chose, He has shortened the days. If anyone says to you, 'Look here is the Christ! Look, here He is!' Do not believe it. There will arise false Christs and false prophets and will give signs and wonders so as to deceive, if possible, the elect. You listen. I have told you all things beforehand. 14-23

In the previous section they were told to stand firm, while they hold onto faith, it is now time to physically flee. The abomination of desolation is the sign to run. Regardless of what is going on, that is the time to leave Jerusalem. The abomination is spoken of in Daniel and there have been several abominations, yet the one is in reference to the fall of Jerusalem. One theory is that at 67 AD John of Gilshala set himself up as a false priest who desecrated the sacrificial system just before Rome destroyed the city. The Christians during this time flee to the regions of the Decopolis, just as Jesus warned. As has happened many times false leaders will arise and must not be followed.

But in those days, after that tribulation, 'the sun will be darkened and the moon not give its light, and the stars will be falling out of the heavens, and the powers in heaven will be shaken. Then they will see the Son of Man coming in the clouds with power and great glory, and then He will send the angels and will gather together his elect from the four winds and from the ends of the earth to the ends of heaven. 24-27

This section quoting Joel demonstrates cataclysmic collapse with the return of Christ, who returns to gather His elect. It appears to be completely different from the preceding passages about running for the mountains. There is nowhere to run from angels gathering the elect.

Now learn the parable of the fig tree. When branches become tender and leaves come out, you know summer is near. So when you see these things coming to pass you know that the end is near, at the door. Truly I say to you, this generation will not have passed away until these things shall have taken place. Heaven and earth will pass away, but My words will not pass away. 28-31

The signs of the fig tree in spring are obvious, so when the abomination comes it will be obvious.. This passage seems to refer back to the destruction of Jerusalem when the abomination sign is clear and is the stimulus to flee which would happen during their lifetime some forty years after Jesus spoke.

Concerning the day or the hour, no one knows, not even the angels in heaven, nor the Son, but the Father. Look! Watch! You do not know when that time is. It is like a man going on a journey having left his house and given his servants authority. Each one has his work, with the one at the door to keep watch. Therefore watch! You do not know when the master of the house comes. At evening, at midnight, when the

> *rooster crows, or at dawn. Yet, if he comes suddenly, do not let him find you sleeping. Now what I say to you, I say to all. Watch! 32-37*

"The day or hour" is now unknown referring to the return of Christ on the clouds and the angels gathering the elect. For centuries, many false teachers and cults have attempted to predict the time of Christ's return. Jesus is claiming that even He and the angels do not know when it will happen and they are fulfilling the prophecy! The command is to persevere as a disciple and to "keep watch." To be alert and ready for Christ's return. The command to keep watch will become a theme in the next chapter.

CHAPTER FOURTEEN

The Passover and the feast of unleavened bread is two days away. The chief priests and scribes were seeking a deceitful way to seize Him to kill Him. Yet, they were saying to each other, "Not during the feast or the people will riot."

He was in Bethany in the house of Simon the leper. As He was eating, a woman came with an alabaster jar of very expensive fragrant oil made of pure nard. She broke it and poured it on His head. Some were angry saying "Why this waste of fragrant oil? It could have been sold for nearly a year's wages and the money given to the poor?" And they were scolding her. And Jesus said, "Leave her alone, why are you troubling her? She has done a beautiful thing for Me. For the poor you will always have with you. You can help them whenever you desire, but you will not always have Me. She did what she could. She anointed My body beforehand for my burial. Truly I tell you, wherever the gospel will be preached throughout the world what she has done will be spoken in remembrance of her."

And Judas Iscariot, one of the twelve, went to the chief priests to betray Him to them. They rejoiced and promised to give him money, so he was looking for an opportunity to betray Him. 1-11

These three stories create a major contrast. The utterly corrupt religious leaders who are attempting to destroy Jesus in a deceitful way, followed by the woman who is the perfect example of sacrificial service, and concluding with one of the twelve Apostles seeking to betray Him. All those who should be examples of servant leadership are the villains, with the anonymous woman (criticized by His disciples) is the example of faith and sacrifice. While the leaders say they will not try to kill Jesus this week during the feast, it just so happens that Jesus' hour to give His life is near. It is God's plan that He be the Passover lamb for all people.

And on the first day of unleavened bread when they were to sacrifice the Passover lamb, the disciples said to Him, "Where do you want us to go prepare the Passover for You to eat?" He sent two disciples and says to them, "Go into the city and you will meet a man carrying a pitcher of water. Follow him. Say to the owner of the house he enters, "The teacher says, where is My guest room where I may eat the Passover with My disciples?" And he will show you a large upper room furnished and ready. Make preparations for us there." The disciples went into the city and found it as He said to them and they prepared the Passover. That evening He came with the twelve.

12-17

Preparing for the Passover was a major undertaking. The disciples are concerned that it is happening today and they have not even started preparations. How would they find a prepared place now that Jerusalem was filled with pilgrims from all over the region to celebrate Passover? Jesus gives an odd prophecy concerning stalking an unknown man who would be carrying a water jar (thought to be Mark himself, with Passover being in his home). Again, simply demonstrating God is in charge of what must take place as they celebrate Passover.

> *As they were eating, Jesus said to them, "Truly I say to you, one of you will betray Me, one who is eating with Me." They were sorrowful and said one by one, "Surely not I!" "It is one of the twelve, one who is dipping in the same bowl as Me. Yes, the Son of Man goes just as it is written about Him, but woe to the man who betrays the Son of Man. Better for him had he not been born."*
>
> *As they were eating, He took bread, and spoke a blessing. He broke it and gave it to them saying, "This is My body." Taking the cup and giving thanks and giving it to them they all drank from it. He said to them, "This is My blood of the covenant which is being poured out for many. Truly, I say to you, I will not drink again of the fruit of the vine until the day when I drink it anew in the kingdom of God. And having sung a hymn, they went out to the Mount of Olives.*
> *18-26*

Again, Jesus knows precisely what will happen. The meal

that is supposed to celebrate thanksgiving and unity is the moment when greed and betrayal will arise. Even then, Jesus will continue serving the meal and He will become the final fulfillment of Passover. The celebration of God delivering Israel from Egypt is now the celebration of the new covenant initiated by His sacrifice which is now so near that this is His last meal before the crucifixion.

> *And Jesus says to them, "All will fall away. For it has been written, 'I will strike the shepherd and the sheep will scatter' But after I have risen, I will go ahead of you into Galilee" And Peter was saying to Him, "Even if all fall away, I will not!" And Jesus says to him, "Truly, I say to you, that you, now, this night, before the rooster crows twice, will deny Me three times." He kept insisting, "Even if I have to die with You, I will never deny You!" Likewise all the others said the same. 27-31*

While Judas would betray, all of them will fall away. Quoting Zechariah, the shepherd who has been leading and teaching will be struck and the followers will flee. Peter in boldness makes the promise that even if everyone else flees, that he will not. Yet again, Jesus' words will be fulfilled. Jesus gives him in exact detail how he will deny Him. Peter along with the others claim they are with Him to the death.

> *They come to a place named Gethsemane. And He says to His disciples, "Sit here while I pray." He takes Peter, James, and John with Him and He begins to be exceedingly distressed and troubled. And He says to them, "My soul is deep with sorrow to the point of death. Stay here and keep watch."*

> *Going a little further, He fell on the ground and was praying if possible this hour might pass from Him. And He was saying, "Abba, Father, all things are possible with You. Take this cup away from Me, but not what I will, but what You will!" And He comes and finds them sleeping, and He says to Peter, "Simon, are you asleep? Were you not able to watch with Me one hour? Watch and pray that you may not enter into temptation. The spirit is willing, but the flesh is weak."*
>
> *Going away again, He prayed the same thing. Again, returning He found them sleeping, for their eyes were heavy. They did not know what to say to Him. He comes the third time and says to them, "Are you still sleeping and resting? It's fulfilled, the hour has come. Look, the Son of Man is delivered into the hands of sinful men. Arise, let's go! Look, My betrayer draws near." 32-42*

As they walk through Gethsemane, a garden in the Mount of Olives just outside the city, Jesus tasks them to watch and pray. We then see the devastation in Jesus' soul, both described by Mark and in Jesus' own words. As He falls to the ground, He affirms the Father's complete control of the situation and Jesus affirms His complete obedience to the Father. Yet, Jesus still prays that another way would satisfy the Father's plan.

As Jesus returns to them, they are sleeping when they should be watching and praying. This lack of preparedness sets the stage for the fleeing and Peter's imminent denial. If they cannot pray during this time, how would they win the battle when temptation comes? Jesus comes to them three times finding them sleeping.

It is interesting that Jesus keeps checking on them, when He knows they are about to betray Him. Upon His third checkup, He knows the Father's answer is that the hour has come. He says, "It is fulfilled" which could be translated "It is paid," speaking of the money transfer. Once Jesus knows there is no other way, He rouses the disciples and walks directly and fearlessly toward Judas.

> *Immediately, as Jesus said this, Judas, one of the twelve, along with a crowd with swords and clubs came from the chief priests, scribes, and elders. He had given them a sign saying, "Whoever I kiss is the one, seize Him and lead Him away under guard." Immediately coming up to Him, he says, "Teacher." And he kissed Him.*
>
> *Laying hands on Him they seized Him. Then one standing by having drawn a sword struck the servant of the high priest, cutting off his ear. Jesus said to them, "As if I am a robber you come out to take me with swords and clubs? Every day I was with you in the temple teaching and you did not take Me. But it is so the scriptures may be fulfilled." Then they all deserted Him and fled. A young man following Him wearing nothing but a sheet, as the men lay hold of him, he left the sheet behind and fled naked. 43-52*

Judas comes with a mob sent by the religious leaders who have been trying to kill Jesus since chapter 3. The leaders have not acted before because of their constant fear of the crowd, but now in the middle of the night this crowd is their own gang of thugs with Judas taking the lead. His hypocrisy is boundless, identifying Jesus with a kiss.

We know from other gospels that Peter is the one who cut off the ear of the high priest's servant. This is Peter making good on his promise, after his naps, he is ready to fight to the death. Likely outnumbered and only being a fisherman rather than a swordsman, he couldn't have thought he would survive the battle. Yet, no other violence ensues at the moment. Jesus points out the same hypocrisy here that He has been calling out since the beginning, yet now their deceit is enfolded into God's plan for the crucifixion.
Then it happens, they all flee. Jesus is alone. The one fleeing naked has traditionally been identified as Mark.

> *They led Jesus away to the high priest. All the chief priests, scribes, and elders come together. Peter followed Him from afar to the courtyard of the high priest. He was sitting with the guards warming himself by the fire. The chief priests and all the Sanhedrin were seeking for testimony to put Him to death but could not find any. Many were giving false testimony, but they did not agree. Some came and were giving false testimony against Him saying, "We heard Him saying, "I will destroy this man-made temple and in three days build another one not made by man." Even then their testimonies did not agree.*
>
> *The high priest stood up among them and questioned Jesus saying, "Are You not going to answer? What are these testimonies against you?" But Jesus remained silent, he gave no answer. Again the high priest questioned Him saying, "Are You the Christ, the Son of the Blessed One?" Jesus said, "I Am. And you will*

> *see the Son of Man sitting at the right hand of power and coming on the clouds of heaven." The high priest tore his clothes and says, "Why would we need more witnesses? You heard the blasphemy! What do you think?" And they all condemned Him to death. Some began to spit on Him, and to cover His face and hit him and say, "Prophesy!" The officers slapped Him. 53-65*

Those who sent the mob are safely tucked away at the high priest's home. Peter has fled, but follows now unsure of what to do. The leaders try to put on a trial, but every rule of law is broken. They must finish condemning Him before the crowds come in the morning.

Then the high priest asks the question about His identity. Jesus has been keeping His identity partially hidden, even when Peter identified Him as the Christ, Jesus told them to keep quiet. He told the demons not to tell who He was. It is now when questioned by the high priest, when He will give His life for the world that He reveals completely and totally who He is to the highest ranking member of Judaism. This is the climactic moment. Him claiming to be the messiah, the Christ is a crime punishable by death. He even claims He will come again in the future from heaven to rule and judge. This sets the leaders against Him and they physically attack.

> *As Peter was below in the courtyard, a servant girl of the high priest came and seeing Peter warming himself, looking at him she says, "You were also with Jesus of Nazareth." But he denied it saying, "I do not know or even understand what you are talking about." He went out on the entryway and the rooster*

> *crowed. Again, the servant girl seeing him says to those standing by, "This is one of them." But, again he denied.*
>
> *After a little while, those standing by were saying to Peter, "Truly, you are also one of them for you are a Galilean." But he began to curse and swear, "I do not know the man you are talking about!" Immediately the roosters crowed the second time. Peter remembered the word that Jesus had said to him, "Before the rooster crows twice you will deny me three times. And he broke down and wept. 66-72*

While Jesus has revealed His identity and has been condemned, Peter is hiding his identity to, of all people, a servant girl. There would be no more person of less importance of status than this girl. But Peter has given into temptation. He lost the battle of prayer and his quick swordplay was also a losing fight. He is now in a moment of spiritual defeat. His first response to the girl is that he is not even aware of Jesus' existence. The rooster crows and he moves out and is followed by the girl who now tells the people around and denies again. Then the people standing around say it again, and the language is very severe saying that he is calling down curses upon himself and swearing. He is supposed to be the one who would be a witness for Jesus during the accusation just inside the building he is next to, yet he denies. The second crow brings him back to reality and he remembers the words of Jesus.

CHAPTER FIFTEEN

Early in the morning, the chief priest held counsel with the elders and scribes and the whole Sanhedren. They bound Him and led Him away to Pilate. Pilate questioned Him, "You are the king of the Jews?" Answering Jesus says, "You say so." And the chief priests were accusing Him of many things. Pilate, again, began to question Him saying, "Are you not going to answer? Look how many things they accuse you of? But Jesus said nothing, and Pilate is amazed.

During the feast he would release one prisoner to them who they requested. There was a rebel named Barabbas who committed murder in an uprising. The crowd cried out asking to do as he usually did. Pilate answered them saying, "Do you want me to release the king of the Jews?" For he knew it was out of envy the chief priests had handed Him over. But the chief priest stirred up the crowd so that Barrabus would be released instead.

Again, Pilate was saying to them, "What then do you want me to do with the one you call the King of the Jews?" They cried out "Crucify Him!" Pilate says, "Why? What evil has He committed?" But they vehemently shouted, "Crucify Him!" Pilate, wanting to satisfy the crowd, released Barabbas to them and had Jesus flogged and delivered Him to be crucified 1-15

Pilate was the governor and the one with the authority to kill or release Jesus. Pilate however, because of previous problems, was trying to regain his reputation among his superiors. He is trying to maintain order among a group that is typically volatile. Calling Jesus the "King of the Jews" is a sarcasm targeted at the religious leaders.

Pilate is now amazed that Jesus is silent, that He is not defending himself. Pilate hopes the crowd will ask to have Jesus released since it was a tradition for Pilate to release a prisoner. He knows the leaders are simply jealous, but the moment is right and the crowd is out for self-centered gain. In an act of anti-leadership Pilate becomes a crowd pleaser by releasing Barrabus and having Jesus flogged and crucified.

The soldiers led him away into the palace, that is the Praetorium, and they called together the whole guard. They dressed Him in purple, and twisted together a crown of thorns and put on Him. They began to salute Him, "Hail King of the Jews!" They kept hitting His head with a staff and spitting on Him, and falling on their knees they were kneeling to Him. After they had mocked Him, they took off the purple clothes and put His clothes on Him. And they led Him out to crucify Him.

> *They forced a passerby named Simon of Cyrene, coming from the countryside, the father of Alexander and Rufus, to carry His cross. They brought Him to Golgotha, which means "place of a skull." They offered Him wine mixed with myrrh, but He did not take it. And they crucified Him, dividing his clothes, casting lots, to decide what each would take.*
>
> *It was 9:00 a.m. when they crucified Him. There was an inscription with the crime against Him. It read, "THE KING OF THE JEWS" They crucified two robbers with Him, one on His right and one on His left. Those passing by blasphemed Him, shaking their heads at him saying, "Look, you saying you would destroy the temple and build it in three days, save Yourself, come down from the cross!" Likewise the chief priests and scribes mocked Him among themselves, saying, "He saved others, but He cannot save Himself. Let this Christ, the King of Israel, come down from the cross that we might see and believe!" And those being crucified with Him were insulting Him. 16-32*

In just a few sentences Jesus is led away, mocked, makes the journey to Golgotha, is crucified, and mocked again. While he underwent unbearable physical pain and spiritual separation from the Father, Mark's account of the crucifixion is not only brief, but highlights the shame and mocking of Jesus. While Mark gives the most detail of the miracles and exorcisms with great detail, he treats the crucifixion differently. There is nothing about pain, nails, or even blood. Jesus is the forsaken one, the object of ridicule, the one scorned. Ruthlessly mocked by both the guards who represent the Gentile rejection, scorned by the crowd, mocked by the religious leaders, and even insulted by those hanging from crosses next to Him. The unknown Simon of Cyrene is the only positive example in the crucifixion. As Jesus taught in chapter 9, Simon has literally taken up the cross and followed.

> *At noon, darkness came over the whole land until 3:00 p.m. At 3:00, Jesus cried out in a loud voice, "Eloi, Eloi, Lema Sabachthani?" Which translated is "My God, My God, Why have You forsaken Me?" Some standing by hearing Him, said, "Look, He calls Elijah." One ran and filled a sponge with wine vinegar, putting it on a reed to give Him a drink saying, "Wait, leave Him alone, let's see if Elijah will come take Him down." Jesus, making a loud cry, breathed His last. The veil of the temple was torn in two from top to bottom. The centurion, standing facing Him, saw how He took His last breath and said, "Truly, this man was the Son of God!" 33-39*

Here darkness breaks over the land and Jesus shouts out in his native Aramaic about God forsaking Him. It is the first line of Psalm 22, with the next sentence verse of the Psalm reading, "Why are you so far from saving me, from the words of my groaning? O my God, I cry by day, but you do not answer, and by night, but I find no rest." (Psalm 22:1b-2 ESV.) It was a cry to the Father expressing as the sin of the world is placed upon Him.

Everyone had forsaken, scattered, plotted, falsely accused, or denied Him by now, but it was the agony of tearing away from the Father that is the agony of the cross. The word "Elio" is almost identical in Aramaic to the name "Elijah."

One mistakes His cry to God as calling for Elijah. One brings a pain killer, wine vinegar, but Jesus will not be drugged. He will be fully alert. The veil is likely a symbol of tearing the barrier between God and people.

Jesus breathes His last and the Centurion is the closest witness to the last breath. He had seen many people die, yet this outsider, the symbol of the power against Him, is the first man to proclaim that Jesus is the Son of God. Now, as it will be proclaimed throughout the ages, it will be with the full understanding that the Son of God, the messiah, died on a cross.

> *There were also women looking on from a distance, Mary Magdalene, Mary the mother of James the younger, and Joseph and Salome. These women had followed Him in Galilee and ministered to Him and many others coming up with Him to Jerusalem.*
>
> *It was evening, preparation day before the Sabbath. Joseph of Arimathea, a prominent member of the council, who was also waiting for the Kingdom of God, boldly went to Pilate to ask for the body of Jesus. Pilate, surprised that Jesus was already dead, called to the centurion to ask if He already died. Hearing from the centurion that it was so, He granted the body to Joseph. Having bought a linen cloth, he took down the body of Jesus, and wrapped Him in the cloth and laid Him in a tomb which was cut out of rock. He rolled a stone to the door of the tomb. Mary Magdalene and Mary the mother of Joseph were watching where He was laid. 34-47*

Ironically a member of the Sanhedrin, the group that had

plotted His death, comes and boldly asks for Jesus' body. He is not ashamed to break ranks with the council and offers his tomb for Jesus. He is likely disowned by all His associates after this act, but again, it is the surprise of who has faith and who does not. Throughout the gospel Jesus has found faith among people we do not expect, while the people who should have it, do not.

CHAPTER SIXTEEN

After the Sabbath, Mary Magdalene and Mary the mother of James and Salome brought spices having come to anoint Him. Very early on the first day of the week, at sunrise, they come to the tomb. They were saying among themselves, who will roll away the stone for us?

Looking up they see the very large stone had been rolled away. Having entered the tomb they saw a young man on the right clothed in white and they were greatly amazed. He says to them, "Do not be amazed, Jesus the Nazarene you seek, having been crucified, He is risen. He is not here! Look at the place where they laid Him. But go and say to His disciples and to Peter that He goes before you into Galilee. You will see Him there as He said to you." Leaving, they fled from the tomb. Trembling and amazed they spoke to no one for they were afraid. 1-8

The ladies are there, the same ones who were at the crucifixion. They had to come back after the Sabbath to prepare the body. They are having a conversation on the way to the tomb that lets us know they were not expecting a resurrection. As they enter the tomb the young man says, “Do not be amazed.” Yet this is the most amazing miracle to ever happen. Jesus has not only been raised, He has already gone ahead of them into Galilee as promised. The young man, assumed to be an angel, sends them to go and tell others, they get to be the first ones to share the news. At first they go out and say nothing out of fear.

At this point, the original ending of Mark is unknown. Most Bibles today have it bracketed with an explanation. The women leaving in fear is an odd way to end the gospel. Very early on perhaps by the middle of the second century other endings were added to keep Mark from ending so abruptly. The endings are in a different style and are verses from the other gospels and the book of Acts. Most importantly is the ascension of Jesus into heaven and the Great Commission to go into the world and preach the gospel. Other passages are more problematic. Drinking poison we see nowhere else. We see Paul get bit by a snake and it does not harm him in Acts 28:3-6, yet there is no command for such a practice. Jesus appearing in a different form appears to be the two on the road to Emmaus from Luke 24.

Yet again, regardless of the ending of the text, the resurrection is clear. The book of Acts takes over the story line of the message of Jesus going forth. The abrupt ending also may be a spiritual prompt to the reader to be confronted with the call to pick up the spiritual baton and live a life of faith for the spiritual chapter in one’s own life. It is the life of the readers and doers of the word that the story of faith continues.

While the ending of the book is not certain, the message of the gospel is clear and compelling. Jesus establishes His identity as the messiah and son of God. He is the king who brings a radically different kingdom that can only be entered through a childlike faith. Those entering the kingdom by faith can only live in it as disciples who bear fruit and follow unashamed. His disciple is in prayer, watchful, and humbly serving one another as they share the faith with others, making new disciples.

ACKNOWLEDGEMENT

I have been influenced by so many who have invested in the gospel from Jesus day till now. Missionaries, teachers, pastors, parents, whatever role people have filled in the body of Christ and been faithful, I am thankful for them.

To my seminary professors who enlightened me, ministry mentors who awakened me, faculty at Grace University who sharpened me, students who invigorated me, church members at Safe Harbor Christian Church, where I pastor, who serve with me, and my family who supports me.

Thanks to Rena Yeager for turning the document into "book ready." Check out her books at renabellyeager.com.

Thanks also to Kendall Unrau for creating a great cover.

ABOUT THE AUTHOR

Richard Ramsey, Phd

Richard (Rich) Ramsey started reading and teaching the Bible in the mid 1990's. To become equipped to teach as a life calling, he completed a Master of Divinity and PhD at The Southern Baptist Theological Seminary in Louisville KY. For the next fourteen years he was a professor of Christian Education & Ministry at Grace University in Omaha, Nebraska, teaching and mentoring students to minister God's Word in a plethora of settings. Since 2017, he has pastored Safe Harbor Christian Church in Memphis, Indiana.

He and Deana, his wife, are parents to five children and reside in Henryville, Indiana. They enjoy engaging with the community, hosting, track season, and juggling schedules. Yet, most of all they become inspired when they see people make faith in Christ the priority of life.

This book is a companion piece to the Gospel of Mark: Live – the live dramatic performance of the entire gospel from memory performed by Rich. As people encounter the spoken gospel, this short book explains the overall themes and specific meanings of passages. If interested in more information about the live performance you can contact Rich at pastorrichramsey@gmail.com.

NOTES

NOTES

www.ingramcontent.com/pod-product-compliance
Lightning Source LLC
LaVergne TN
LVHW090529110826
845146LV00003B/1035

* 9 7 9 8 9 9 5 0 0 2 8 0 2 *